Multiprocessor Methods for Computer Graphics Rendering

Computer Science Publishing Program

Multiprocessor Methods for Computer Graphics Rendering

Scott Whitman

Lawrence Livermore National Laboratory
Livermore, California

Jones and Bartlett Publishers
Boston   London

Editorial, Sales, and Customer Service Offices
Jones and Bartlett Publishers
20 Park Plaza
Boston, MA 02116

Jones and Bartlett Publishers International
P.O. Box 1498
London W6 7RS
England

About the cover: The tree dataset was generated using Eric Haines' SPD database and
rendered at a resolution of 640 by 484 pixels. The tree contains approximately 850,000
polygons and was rendered on 96 processors of a BBN TC2000 in 8.8 seconds (including
specular highlights and stochastic sampling for anti-aliasing).

Library of Congress Cataloging-in-Publication Data

Not available at press time.

ISBN   0-86720-229-7

Printed in the United States of America

96 95 94 93 92   10 9 8 7 6 5 4 3 2 1

To Carol,

who was not there to share the past,
but with whom I shall enjoy the future

Table of Contents

Preface

Parallel computing and computer graphics are currently two of the hottest topics in computer science. It is only natural that a merging of these two fields has now occurred in hardware architectures as well as software algorithms. This text explores a number of methods which can be used on current generation commercial multiprocessors to perform computer image synthesis. The emphasis here is on image space rendering methods since these types of algorithms will likely get the most use in the day to day work environment.

The subject matter of computer image synthesis is over 20 years old, dating back to Warnock's and Watkins' rendering algorithms, along with Gouraud's lighting model. Since then, many refinements have been developed which use advanced hardware and software techniques to hasten the rendering computation. The availability and price/performance ratio of commercial multiprocessors makes them attractive for development of general purpose computer graphics algorithms. When parallel computer architectures became commercially available in the mid-1980s, the sequential programs that had been previously developed for computer graphics rendering were in need of a re-evaluation for a parallel context. In addition, it was questioned whether new and completely different rendering programs would be required for use on these computers. In this book, we examine previous and current solutions to the computer image generation problem presented by a variety of researchers. Several of these solutions, along with a number of newly developed algorithms by the author, are analyzed according to their performance on a scalable multiprocessor.

The problem of quickly generating three-dimensional synthetic imagery has remained challenging for computer graphics researchers due to the large amount of data which is processed and the complexity of the calculations involved. For instance, in a multiprocessor, one needs to minimize the communication of data between processors so that the majority of the execution time is spent on computations. The large datasets inherent in computer graphics scenery do not lend themselves to ease of partitioning among processors. Tradeoffs between synchronization, load balancing, and communication must be made during algorithm development and refinement in order to effectively utilize the resources available in the system. These issues are discussed in detail in this text with regard to the parallel algorithms which were implemented on the BBN Butterfly family of computers. Although the algorithms were developed for these machines, they could be modified with minimal effort to work on any general purpose multiprocessor. Unfortunately, the time to modify and test the code on a variety of machines would be prohibitive, especially to the degree used in the latter part of this book. It is hoped that the insights presented here along with the various issues raised, and will be informative as both a guide for implementation and a reference to methods of attacking this problem.

In the first chapter of this book, an overview of computer graphics rendering is provided, and the issues that are of importance to the fields of computer graphics and parallel processing are noted. The second chapter provides a historical reference to previous efforts in this field. Each of these is categorized into a taxonomy to indicate what algorithmic methods each work has utilized. Most of this research involved simulations of parallel environments whereas this book provides an analysis of actual implementations on general purpose commercially available multiprocessors. The third chapter analyzes the various multiprocessor architectures with regard to graphics rendering algorithms. In chapter 4, the basis parallel algorithm is presented, along with the procedures used for testing and performance analysis. Chapter 5 includes descriptions and analyses of each of the work decomposition methods which were implemented. The analysis is a scrutiny of a given program's parallel performance which provides information to the reader on exactly why each algorithm performed the way it did. There were two main choices for storing the graphics data in main memory, and these are analyzed in chapter 6. The first is a shared memory paradigm while the second, although using shared memory, takes advantage of local memory on each processor to reduce latency. The results for all of the algorithms are compared on a variety of imagery to convince the reader that the results presented are representative of real world expected performance.

Acknowledgments. This book was originally a doctoral dissertation written and researched while I was at The Ohio State University. My dissertation committee of Richard Parent, P. Sadayappan, and D. Jayasimha helped to guide me through the difficult phases of my research. I am indebted to my committee for the countless hours of useful discussions and comments that they provided me on my dissertation. Others who helped to make my stay at Ohio State that much more rewarding include Scott Dyer, Doug Roble, Manas Mandal, as well as my other colleagues in the Computer and Information Science Department, the Advanced Computing Center for Arts and Design, and the Ohio Supercomputer Center.

This research was conducted over a period of several years and utilized literally thousands of hours of computer time. The author would like to acknowledge the institutions and staff at BBN Advanced Computers, Inc., Argonne National Laboratory, and Lawrence Livermore National Laboratory for allowing their machines to be used for benchmarking and testing purposes. Individuals deserving special recognition for their assistance include: Ed Forbes, John Price, Linda Woods, and Eugene Brooks.

Scott R. Whitman

1

Introduction

High quality computer graphics imagery is used in a wide variety of fields in society today. Most people are familiar with the entertainment uses of computer graphics which span the artistic realm and include two-dimensional imagery using paintbox systems, three-dimensional surreal scenes for aesthetic prints, and 2D and 3D animation sequences for use in the video and film industry. There are many major motion pictures which rely on computer graphics rendering to achieve cost effective special effects. The quality of this imagery has risen to such a high level that the public is accustomed to seeing on a regular basis computer generated commercials of photorealistic caliber. In addition, applications such as CAD/CAM, finite element modeling, flight simulation, and molecular modeling use computer graphics to aid in the visualization of scientific and industrial data. The demand for higher quality images from these applications has grown as computer time has become less expensive. Even though faster computers are now available in reference to the past, the time to generate a typical image has not really decreased due to the more elaborate imagery required. Deering [Deer88] noted that "an increase in graphics performance is more likely to cause users to display more complex objects, rather than the same objects faster." A computer graphics display algorithm must be able to handle this highly complex imagery in an efficient manner. One solution to this problem involves utilizing parallel computer architectures to render the graphics image. If an efficient software algorithm is employed on this type of machine, performance will increase with the number of processors added to the system.

This book examines techniques which utilize parallel processing to accelerate the computations necessary for rendering three-dimensional computer graphics scenes. The most promising algorithms are developed and quantitatively compared under a variety of circumstances to ascertain which has the highest performance.

The basic problem in computer image synthesis of 3D scenes is outlined in the first section of this chapter. Here, the components of a computer graphics display algorithm are described. The terms *hidden surface removal* and *rendering* are defined in the context of a computer graphics display program. The second section presents a brief overview of the research which has been done in the area of developing parallel computer graphics rendering techniques. This research can be broadly grouped into two categories: hardware and software based solutions. The hardware based solutions typically involve designing custom VLSI chips to transform and display data in near real-time. *Real-time* is a term used to describe calculations which can proceed within the update rate for a single frame on a CRT monitor, typically 30 frames per second. Software solutions use high performance advanced computer architectures to achieve fast computer graphics renderings. The goals of each of these methods are described in some detail in this section. The third section outlines the area of research which this book covers. In this section, the context of this work in both the parallel processing and computer graphics communities is stated. Finally, the fourth section provides an overview of the rest of the text.

1.1. Problem Description

Computer graphics imagery can serve many purposes, but the basic computer program used to generate these images is the same, regardless of the intended application. The input data consists of a set of objects which are described both geometrically and topologically, using a polygonal format. Various scene parameters are also input to describe the lights, shading, color, and other information regarding how the objects should appear in the computer synthesized scene. All data is input as x, y, z floating point variables. The input datasets are assumed to contain closed planar polygons. The output of a graphics display algorithm is a rendering of a three-dimensional scene, taking into account realistic lighting and object attributes. This output is an image in the form of picture elements (pixels) which may be displayed immediately on a frame buffer color monitor or stored on hard disk for later display. A *frame buffer* is a dynamic memory collection of pixels containing red, green, and blue components. Each pixel component is usually 8 bits deep allowing for a choice of 256^3 or approximately 16 million colors.

In general, a computer graphics display algorithm which generates images of three-dimensional data consists of the following phases:

1. Read-in polygonal data from disk.
2. Transform data from object space to eye space.
3. Clip and perform perspective projection of the data.
4. Remove hidden surfaces so only displayable surfaces are seen.
5. Render surface data using an illumination model.
6. Calculate special visual effects such as anti-aliasing or texture mapping.
7. Write pixel data to the frame buffer for display or to a file for storage.

The overall algorithm is shown in detail in figure 1.1. The top diagram indicates the world space three-dimensional view of a sphere dataset composed of quadrilateral polygons. The sphere is initially described in its own 3D coordinate system (object space). The scene as a whole consists of a collection of objects in 3D space relative to each other. In addition, an eye point and light sources are present in the scene (world space or eye space). In order for the graphics program to display the scene on a two-dimensional screen, each object must be transformed to screen space and (if necessary) clipped to the borders of the screen. The middle diagram is the same sphere after 3D to 2D transformations, clipping, and perspective operations have been applied. The bulk of the work in the program occurs in the rendering phase. This amounts to taking into account the position of the eye and each light source in relation to the objects in the scene, and then accurately displaying the objects according to their surface geometry. Incorporated here are such operations as hidden surface removal, illumination modeling, anti-aliasing, and other visual effects.

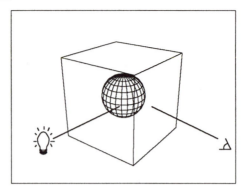

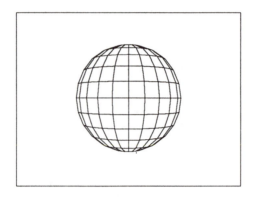

Figure 1.1: Graphics rendering pipeline

These operations are elaborated upon in the sub-sections that follow. This process is shown in the bottom diagram as the final rendered and shaded image which takes into account the location of the light source, object, and eye position.

The problem domain of this book focuses primarily on the *tiling* portion of a graphics display algorithm (steps 4, 5, and 6). Methods to speed up both the front end (reading in, transforming of data) as well as the back end (writing out pixels) of the program are also investigated. The assumption here is that the nature of the input and output is unique to each application, while tiling is the same for the majority of applications. Because the tiling operations constitute the bulk of the computation in this type of program, it is worthwhile to concentrate one's efforts on this section of a graphics rendering algorithm. Steps 4, 5, and 6 are described in more detail next.

1.1.1. Hidden Surface Removal

Hidden surface removal consists of determining which surface element in the synthetic 3D scene is closest to the observer for each pixel on a CRT screen. There are a variety of techniques for solving this problem, and most take advantage of some form of coherence in the image in order to reduce the amount of computation. In Sutherland, Sproull, and Schumacker's landmark paper [Suth74], graphical coherence is defined as "the extent to which the environment or the picture of it is locally constant." For instance, scan line coherence refers to the fact that successive lines of pixels do not differ greatly in the data displayed, so that incremental calculations can be used to achieve faster processing. Sutherland et al. point out that "all of the [display] algorithms capitalize on various forms of coherence to reduce to manageable proportions the work of sorting." The exploitation of image coherence in a parallel setting poses a challenging problem. The use of coherence reduces the amount of computation in a sequential machine by using results from previously computed parameters when generating new values. The independent parallel generation of these parameter values in the image implies redundant recomputation and the loss of coherence. The tradeoff between parallelism and coherence is an important issue that is studied here.

1.1.2. Rendering and Special Effects

Rendering is a method for displaying polygonal or bicubic patch surfaces on a frame buffer monitor so that the overall surface geometry is approximated and lighting in the scene is taken into account. Rendering techniques include illumination models such as Gouraud [Gour71] and Phong [Phon75] shading, which are used to simulate smooth surfaces. Using Lambert's law and approximations to the normal vector of the surface at each pixel, the data can be displayed accurately on the screen. Computer graphics special effects add realism to a computer generated scene. Some of these include: calculating refractions of transparent objects, modeling of wrinkled surfaces (bump mapping), applying texture to a surface (texture mapping), and accounting for shadows in a scene.

Anti-aliasing is another added visual effect which removes the jagged or staircase edges which appear at surface boundaries due to discrete sampling of the analog dataset. Both rendering and special effects are closely tied because the addition of visual features normally occurs during the rendering process. Current display methods incorporate advanced rendering and visual effects as an integral part of the algorithm. The complexity of these computations in most cases overrides those necessary for hidden surface removal. Any techniques used to speed up the image generation process must concentrate heavily on the rendering and visual effects stages.

In the next section, the background on a number of hardware and software graphics techniques is given.

1.2. Overview of Accelerated Rendering Techniques

Although significant work has been done in the past regarding the sequential computer graphics image generation problem, it is necessary to re-investigate this problem to see what changes or alternate approaches are necessary for parallel implementation. Work in this area has centered around both hardware based graphics workstations and software solutions for parallel machines.

Numerous companies have developed graphics superworkstations which incorporate special purpose chips along with multiple processors to achieve a high performance visual computing system. Initial developments in this area involved the use of special purpose graphics terminals which manipulated wire-frame images in real-time. Wire-frame imagery only shows the outline of the dataset surfaces and makes use of phases 1 through 4 given in the beginning of this section. Using today's technology, more sophisticated machines can generate smoothed surface representations in near real-time to aid in visualizing data. The term "real-time" generally refers to an update rate of at least 10 frames per second (fps). Standard video update rate is 30 fps while film is 24 fps.

Commercial machines of this type include the Apollo DN10000VS [Kirk90], the Silicon Graphics 4D VGX [Haeb90], the Stellar Graphics Supercomputer GS1000 [Apga88], and the Ardent Titan [Died88]. All of these machines support parallelism with typically up to 4 processors, while the Stellar and Ardent architectures employ parallel processing at both the MIMD (multiple instruction, multiple data path) and SIMD (single instruction, multiple data path) levels. MIMD refers to the fact that each processor is executing a set of instructions asynchronously from other processors. SIMD refers to a central processor controlling execution or to a vector pipeline architecture. In addition, fast rendering engine processors are coupled with the frame buffer in these machines to achieve high speed generation of images. The Silicon Graphics and Apollo machines support anti-aliasing and texture mapping. The Apollo DN10000VS uses quadratic interpolation to help alleviate Mach bands, although this technique is not quite as good as true Phong shading. Mach bands (see [Roge85]) can occur when the smooth surface interpolation in the illumination model is not an accurate representation of the actual surface. The Silicon Graphics 4D VGX has what is called an "accumulation buffer." This buffer allows such features as motion blur, soft shadows, depth of field, and anti-aliasing to be performed on a polygonal database. Motion blur smooths out the motion of fast moving objects in a scene. Soft shadows provide a smoothing effect to the shadow that simulates a penumbra rather than the typical quick cutoff that is apparent in conventional shadow algorithms. Depth of field simulates the way a camera lens focuses. Other hardware approaches including new chip designs from Schlumberger [Deer88] and IBM [Ghar88] promise high graphics performance for the future.

An example of using a hardware architecture to solve the radiosity problem is given by Baum and Winget [Baum90]. Radiosity is a very computationally expensive technique for visualizing 3D scenes. It is essentially an n^2 problem which involves calculating the diffuse inter-reflection of all surfaces against one another so that the light reflectance of the entire scene is taken into account. In their algorithm, Baum and Winget use the hardware capability of the Silicon Graphics IRIS workstation to perform real-time radiosity. Their algorithm exploits the hardware by using the Z-buffer rendering feature of the IRIS to calculate the form factors in parallel. The Z-buffer is a contiguous memory which holds the Z coordinate value of the closest surface to the viewer for each pixel on the screen. Additional work by Garlick et al. [Garl90] using the IRIS workstation allows one to manipulate very large databases in real-time. This algorithm works by using parallel processing to perform clipping operations necessary to observe the dataset. Although both of these implementations are useful, they do not deal directly with the problem of image generation.

Two architectures which are primarily intended for fast image processing as well as 3D rendering are Pixel Planes and the AT&T Pixel Machine. These machines are designed to offload the graphics calculations from a host computer; they are not intended for use as workstations.

Fuchs et al. [Fuch85] introduced their hardware approach to solving the visualization problem in 1985. Fuchs' team designed Pixel Planes, a parallel architecture containing a processor at every pixel, and a binary tree of adders optimized to solve the equation $F(x,y) = Ax + By + C$ at each pixel. This machine also has hardware support for calculating anti-aliasing, shadows, and texturing.

The AT&T Pixel Machine [Potm89] contains a high performance network of processors with a fine-grained interleaved frame buffer. That is, the frame buffer memory is scattered throughout the processors. This alleviates contention while providing sufficient throughput. It is typically used as a graphics engine which offloads complex rendering calculations from a host computer. With a full configuration of 64 rendering processors, 820 MFLOPS peak performance is attainable. Since this machine is a general purpose graphics machine, software algorithms can be used to take advantage of its characteristics. Although the Pixel Machine can be programmed to handle a number of different graphics display methods, its versatility is limited as a general purpose computer primarily because of the small amount of memory available at each processor (only 64kbytes).

The solutions described above involve integrating a special purpose graphics rendering engine into a high performance workstation or using a hardware assisted graphics accelerator. The first approach yields a near real-time update of polygonal based scenes, which is useful to designers and engineers. The second approach offloads the host for external graphics processing. Even within this realm, the designs suffer limitations. For instance, if anti-aliasing and other features are used, performance degrades dramatically. Quantitative measures of the degradation which occurs when applying anti-aliasing to polygonal models in these machines are not available. True Phong shading is not present in the hardware of any of these machines. Most of the hardware methods employ a Z-buffer type of hidden surface removal algorithm but the data must be stored in the memory of the machine prior to loading into the graphics pipeline. A *Z-buffer* [Catm74] is analogous to the frame buffer except that the z coordinate for a polygon at the given pixel is stored in memory. This is a simple technique used for hidden surface removal. Extremely large datasets are not able to fit into the physical memory of the machine and consequently performance suffers as a result of disk access. As a result of these limitations, a hardware approach is only adequate for interactive use with a small to medium size dataset (typically 10,000 polygons or less). To achieve reasonable performance on large datasets, a parallel software approach to solving the rendering problem is warranted.

The use of a general purpose multiprocessor computer is more cost effective than the specially designed architectures, since this type of machine can be used for non-graphics applications as well. The software method may not have the capability for real-time calculations, but this is not needed in many applications. In addition, a graphics workstation is not capable of the high performance general computing required by applications which demand supercomputer cycles. By integrating the graphics rendering with the application and using the same computer for both simultaneously, it is unnecessary to send the data to a separate machine for graphics rendering. Taking this a step further, we expect that future generation multiprocessors may in fact offer the capability to achieve real-time computer graphics rendering. Following is a description of how this might be used.

For real-time interaction with a complex illumination model, the user is generally limited to a small number of polygons on even the most advanced graphics workstations. With the recent interest in scientific visualization, scientists would like to be able to see their scientific data using real-time interaction, while adjusting their simulation simultaneously. The simulation portion of the code is usually run on a supercomputer class architecture machine. Example applications which require this level of computer power include: molecular dynamics simulations, 3D finite element simulations, and global climate modeling. Massively parallel architectures hold great promise for being able to support applications of this type. In addition, the capability to support real-time interaction of a dense database containing perhaps a million elements is beyond the scope of even the most powerful graphics workstations. Consequently, it is natural to incorporate the graphics rendering operations along with the simulation program in the same computer so that the coupled system can output the graphics image in real-time. This desired interactive environment has come to be known as *simulation steering*.

It is expected that massively parallel architectures will provide the capability to accomplish steering before the end of the 1990s [Upso89]. This book gives insight into how graphics rendering programs will be developed for massively parallel architectures to incorporate this desired feature in the near future. Already, some researchers are looking into using SIMD architectures for such a purpose [Smal89], [Schr91]. Although these machines are likely to provide decent results, it is generally believed that the long term prospects for real-time interactive simulation steering can only be achieved by future generation high performance MIMD computers.

There have been numerous software algorithms presented in the past that have been designed for many different types of advanced architectures. An overview of algorithms of this type is provided by Whitman and Parent [Whit88]. In addition, Crow [Crow88a] provides insight into commercial ventures and other interesting methods used for designing parallel software approaches to display computer graphics images.

Previous work in software algorithms for parallel graphics rendering has primarily concentrated on software simulations or simple ad-hoc solutions. Little work has been done in this area to fully exploit parallel processing at a high level. Some parallel graphics display solutions have dealt with a graphics rendering technique known as ray tracing [Whit80]. *Ray tracing* is a technique which involves sending rays from the observer through each pixel to intersect the objects in the scene.

The advantage of ray tracing is that features such as reflections, refractions, shadowing, motion blur, and depth of field are very easy to implement. On the other hand, an image generated by ray tracing takes several orders of magnitude more time to compute than one which is generated by a conventional image space graphics display algorithm such as the scan line Z-buffer or Watkins' algorithm [Roge85]. Badouel [Bado90] and Green [Gree89] both present a fairly good treatment of ray tracing in parallel on a message passing multiprocessor. Although more work could be done in this area, the analysis in this book is restricted to the more efficient image space rendering algorithms. However, some ray tracing algorithms are presented in the next chapter to illustrate the work that has been done in this area. In the next section, a description of the context of this book in the fields of computer graphics and parallel processing is given.

1.3. Research Context

This text presents an analysis of the most efficient methods for the generation of computer graphics imagery on multiprocessors. Past approaches to parallelizing graphics display algorithms were not designed to take full advantage of the machine architecture. In this book, a variety of techniques are investigated which exploit parallelism in computer graphics image generation. The intention here is to evaluate high performance solutions which perform well on a massively parallel computer. Previously developed serial algorithms are examined for potential parallel extensions. In addition, new parallel approaches to generating computer graphic images are studied to evaluate the methods most suitable for implementation.

A number of different memory referencing strategies are also compared and analyzed on a parallel computer. Jamieson [Jami87] discusses a variety of algorithm and architecture characteristics, and presents guidelines for determining how to fit an algorithm to an architecture. To ascertain the appropriate choice of architecture for implementation purposes, a number of commercial parallel machines are compared in the context of developing a graphics rendering program. A particular computer graphics algorithm may not be well suited to all architectures, however. Therefore, different approaches are categorized according to a number of characteristics in order to obtain a suitable mapping of algorithm to architecture. In evaluating an implementation of a parallel graphics algorithm on a given architecture, various factors that degrade program performance are quantified. These factors help the reader to understand the characteristics specific to the different algorithms.

Most of the previous work in this area by computer graphics researchers involves one of the following procedures: analysis of parallel architectures for graphics, simulation of a parallel machine in software on a von-Neumann architecture, or presentation of an initial software study on a multiprocessor architecture. This text extends the work of others by including detailed comparisons of a number of different algorithmic techniques as implemented on an existing commercial multiprocessor.

1.3.1. Graphics Context

Some issues with regard to this subject matter that various computer graphics specialists have addressed in the past include: 1) SIMD approaches [Dyer87], [Crow88b], [Smal89], [Theo89a], 2) coherence vs. parallelism [Kapl79] (for spatial subdivision algorithms), 3) methods of spatial subdivision [Whel85], [Kapl79], [Hu85], and 4) effect of larger datasets [Whel85]. This is by no means a complete list of the research that has been done in this area. In fact, Burke and Leler [Burk90] present a fairly thorough examination of previous work in this field. The first of these items is not addressed in this text since we are primarily interested in MIMD algorithms here. In chapter 2 we present in more detail the choice of architecture and defer a discussion on this matter to that point. The second item, coherence versus parallelism, is mentioned only briefly in various papers, but has not been analyzed extensively to see to what degree it is worthwhile maintaining graphical coherence in a parallel algorithm. The third item, spatial subdivision methods, has been looked at by the most researchers, but there are other methods that have not been considered. Also, most of the previous work is based on simulations rather than actual implementations. The fourth item, large datasets, is treated fairly completely by Whelan, although his work involves a simulation rather than an implementation.

By comparing implementations, one can determine which parallel task decompositions provide good performance on an actual machine. In these implementations, various parameters such as the number of tasks assigned per processor can be varied to see how performance changes in practice. Memory partitioning and referencing schemes that have not been addressed in any previous work are discussed as well. In a data intensive program such as a graphics display algorithm, the most efficient method for data storage and access cannot be easily determined. This may relate strongly to the type of architecture that the algorithms are implemented on, and should be taken into account as well.

The effect of other parameters such as image complexity and machine characteristics are analyzed. Very little work has taken place on developing a scalable parallel display algorithm. While it may be true that some modifications may be necessary to obtain high performance on upwards of 1024 processors, the goal here is to effectively utilize as little as 2 and as many as 100 or more processors, with no modification in the code.

The work presented in this text can also provide hints to other programmers developing graphics algorithms for parallel environments. For instance, little work has been done in the past regarding radiosity or volume rendering on parallel architectures. Both of these rendering techniques involve large datasets and random memory access. The decomposition and memory referencing schemes developed here may be suitable for extension to these types of applications.

1.3.2. Parallel Computing Context

In relation to how this work fits into a parallel computing context, one should note the following factors. A graphics display program is a fairly detailed program which typically has 5000 or more lines of code. The complexity and size of the data structures used in this application make it fairly difficult to deal with in a straightforward manner. One must determine if a given data item is to be:

1. Read-accessible to all processors.
2. Read-accessible to a limited number of processors.
3. Write-accessible to all processors.
4. Write-accessible to a limited number of processors.

For example, there are several storage methods and issues relevant for a read-accessible data item. The item may be copied to all processors that may reference it, but the overhead of copying as well as excessive memory use may prohibit the usefulness of this approach. It might be possible to regenerate the item each time it is needed on a given processor, but there is a cost associated when this is done. Another alternative could be to remotely reference an item stored in shared memory, but this causes latency problems. These issues are investigated in chapter 5 of this book.

These alternatives bring to light one of the key issues in any computer program: what is the balance between storage and speed that can be best utilized in this implementation? The use of multiple processors re-opens this issue to a whole new set of potential problems. A graphics application uses data items that fit into all four categories, theoretically requiring a decision regarding storage and access for each data item. In reality, it is fairly straightforward for most data to see what storage method would be best. On the other hand, the algorithms do impart some characteristics on memory referencing which may force different design decisions. A balance must be struck in order to obtain good performance under a variety of circumstances.

An in-depth analysis is presented in chapter 4 regarding different issues which relate to parallel programming in the context of this application. These include overheads encountered in a parallel program that are not present in a serial version such as: contention, use of virtual memory in parallel, scheduling, communication, and synchronization, to name a few. These are quantified as to their effect on the overall program performance.

While numerical applications such as LU decomposition and matrix multiplication may involve large amounts of data movement, typically somewhat simpler data structures are used than those required for a graphics display algorithm. The data structures in numerical applications are usually multi-dimensional arrays. In a graphics display algorithm, the polygonal data is initially read into array data structures. After this initial phase, though, the data needs to be maneuvered into complex hierarchical data structures. These can consist of objects, polygon information lists, active edge lists, edge pair data structures, and many other intricate storage mechanisms. For a sequential environment, there is not general agreement among the graphics community about which type of data structure is the most efficient for a particular algorithm. There is certainly room for discussion as to the most suitable data structures for a parallel environment. The parallel architecture influences the decision as to the choice of data structures as well. This decision is especially crucial in a graphics algorithm where there may be a large amount of data needed for any given task. The memory resource in a parallel computer is not infinite, so the data structures must be time and space efficient as well.

One issue not encountered in numerical parallel algorithms is that of parallelism versus graphical coherence. While this is typically a graphics issue, it can be thought of as a parallel computing issue as well, in that different overheads are incurred depending on the task granularity chosen. These overheads are basically due to the lack of coherence induced by separating tasks for execution in parallel. As such, one must investigate to what degree this overhead affects performance insofar as determining the number of tasks to generate.

1.4. Document Overview

In chapter 2, a framework is developed for analyzing parallel graphics display algorithms. A taxonomy of parallel graphics display algorithms is generated in which the possible parallel approaches are categorized into image and object space methods. Previous researchers' work is fit into this taxonomy, and a number of new approaches are examined which could be used to solve the problem. By considering a number of issues relating to parallel algorithm development, it is shown that several types of approaches are worth further consideration.

In chapter 3, a number of multiprocessor architectures are presented in order to determine the one most suitable for implementation. It is easiest to use a previously developed serial display algorithm as a basis for the parallel implementation due to the nature of the architecture chosen. An evaluation of the different MIMD programming models is discussed, including the programming paradigms available on the BBN Butterfly, on which the algorithms were implemented.

Chapter 4 discusses the overall basis graphics display algorithm and how it applies to the chosen architecture. The design decisions which are common to all the implemented parallel algorithms are described. In this way, one can see that it is easy to compare parallel approaches since they are all based on the same code. Finally, the testing procedures which are used in timing the various algorithms on the GP1000 are described.

In chapter 5, a number of different parallel image space subdivision algorithms are presented, based on the pixel decomposition scheme. In this chapter, only the tiling section of the algorithms is compared in order to evaluate the maximum parallelism attainable. For comparison purposes, the size and number of areas is varied. In addition, three different task partitioning schemes are compared. The results are scrutinized, and the overhead percentage factors are determined through experiments in the performance of each parallel algorithm.

In chapter 6, several shared memory storage and referencing schemes are examined. A global storage and referencing scheme is compared to a software caching scheme. Due to the fact that the algorithms for task decomposition affect the memory storage and reference scheme, the overheads involved in implementing each scheme are examined. The various algorithms which are scrutinized in chapter 5 are compared again, but this time the setup cost is included, not just the tiling section cost. Based on this comparison, the task adaptive algorithm utilizing the locally cached memory referencing scheme resulted in the best timings. The issues of parameter variation are investigated in actual implementations of these algorithms. Both the machine and scene parameters can vary, and these variations can change the algorithms' performance.

Chapter 7 presents overall conclusions and discusses future research possibilities.

2

Overview of Parallel Methods for Image Generation

In this chapter, a number of methods which can be used for parallel graphics rendering are discussed and evaluated for their applicability to multiprocessor architectures.

In the first section, a number of factors are presented to serve as a basis for a quantitative analysis of potential algorithms for implementation. The second section presents a historical overview of previous work in the area of parallel graphics algorithms, and these algorithms are categorized and presented in a taxonomy. In addition, new methods are also described and fit into the taxonomy as well.

2.1. Criteria for Evaluation of Parallel Graphics Display Algorithms

A number of parallel approaches to graphics rendering have been developed in the past, and more are certain to be presented in the future. In order to effectively evaluate these different approaches, it is worthwhile analyzing them in terms of a number of important issues including:

1. Level of granularity of task sizes.
2. Nature of algorithm decomposition into parallel tasks.
3. Utilization of parallelism in the display algorithm without significant loss of coherence.
4. Load balancing of tasks.
5. Distribution and access of data through the communication network.
6. Scalability of the algorithm on larger machines.

The interrelations of each of these issues and how they effect the overall parallel algorithm are shown in figure 2.1. These issues are investigated in the context of a number of previous approaches to the parallel image generation problem. They are described in more detail next.

2.1.1. Load Balancing

Load balancing refers to the idea that each processor is used as effectively as its neighbors. This means that in the ideal case, each processor has exactly the same amount of work and will finish its work at the same time as the others. Researchers typically address this issue by developing task partitioning schemes which attempt to create an even load among the processors in one of two ways: either

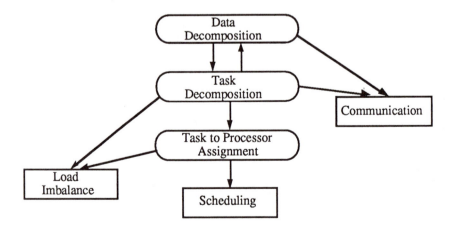

Figure 2.1: Relationship of decomposition methods to parallel overheads

by static assignment of large tasks or by dynamic assignment of smaller tasks.

In the static method of task decomposition, the number of tasks T is typically equal to the number of processors P, and all of the tasks are estimated to take approximately the same amount of time. This requires some additional overhead prior to starting a parallel environment, but the hope is that an even work distribution will result. The advantages of this method are: communication overhead percentage is small due to larger task sizes, task startup overhead is minimized, and scheduling overhead is reduced.

The second method of attacking load balancing is the dynamic approach. In this method, T is determined to be much greater than P, and task assignment to processors proceeds during runtime. A processor continues to work on tasks until no more work is available, at which point it remains idle until all of the processors complete their work. As a result of small task sizes, the idle time is small and will have minimal impact on overall performance. Previous research has shied away from this approach in hardware designs for graphics rendering because it was deemed that the context switching resulted in too much overhead. In a software algorithm, this is not a consideration unless the granularity of these tasks is too fine. If too fine a task granularity is used, it is possible that the time to obtain a new task is too high a percentage of the task execution time, degrading overall program performance. The advantages of the dynamic approach include: 1) task execution time does not need to be determined a priori; 2) load balancing is solved in a dynamic manner; and 3) the time needed to determine what the work will be for each task is much smaller than in the static method. Note that some methods employ a static scheduling of $(T > P)$ tasks as well. However, load balancing is not handled directly in this type of algorithm.

2.1.2. Levels of Granularity

As discussed previously, the parallel decomposition of a computer graphics algorithm can occur at many different levels of granularity. It is necessary to determine the potential number of parallel tasks to identify independent calculations which can be performed in parallel. The partitioning of a display algorithm may be performed in terms of either image space or the object space. A single display algorithm can use any combination of any of these levels to partition the computation. The different levels of granularity are given in table 2.1.

If an algorithm is divided into tasks that are too coarse grained, load balancing will suffer since not enough parallelism is introduced. On the other hand, if too fine a level of granularity is used, then too much context switching will occur which adds time to the parallel program. It seems clear that a medium grain approach is the most viable since it strikes a balance between providing good load balancing and minimizing context switching.

2.1.3. Nature of Parallelism

There are two principal types of methods for decomposing algorithms for a parallel computer--data and functional parallelism. *Data parallelism* refers to dividing up the data among the processors and processing different data segments in parallel. *Functional parallelism* usually involves different threads of control and can be further broken down into operational and procedural levels. *Operational parallelism* refers to concurrency at the basic operations level such as assignment, etc. *Procedural parallelism* is achieved by decomposing the algorithm into sections which are assigned to different processors. *Pipelining* is a form of parallelism that combines features of data level parallelism with functional level parallelism. Although data parallelism is normally associated with SIMD architectures, an MIMD approach can also employ data parallelism in

Table 2.1: Granularity levels in parallelism and computer graphics

Granularity	Program Constructs	Graphics Entities
Very Coarse	programs running on different machines via network	calculation of separate images on different machines at the same time
Coarse	execution of P modules in parallel on P processors	sub-division of scene into objects or groups of objects
Medium	execution of N modules on P processors in parallel where $(N \gg P)$	sub-division of image into sections or sub-division of objects into faces
Fine	parallel computation of loop iterations in SIMD pipeline	parallel processing of groups of pixels or span segments assigning one group per processor
Very Fine	hardware parallelism at instruction level	assignment of processors to calculations at the pixel level

which work is partitioned into parallel components according to the input dataset. Alternative schemes involve using functional parallelism or some combination of functional and data parallelism. The type of parallelism evident in each algorithm is identified as each is discussed since different stages of an algorithm may use different levels of parallelism.

2.1.4. Usage of Graphical Coherence

Recall that graphical coherence is the use of incremental operations rather than recomputation of parameters to hasten the speed of graphics calculations. A major component of every three-dimensional computer graphics display algorithm is sorting data elements in some combination of the x, y, and z directions in three-dimensional space. The advantage of using coherence in this type of algorithm is that sorting can usually be reduced to incremental calculations rather than recomputation of various parameters. Coherence can be examined within computer graphic images at the pixel level, scan line level, area level, or frame level. For example, *scan line coherence* refers to the fact that edges of polygons intersect a number of adjacent scan lines. When edge parameter values such as color or surface normal are calculated for the initial scan line which the edge crosses, the incremental values can be computed and used to update the parameters from one scan line to the next. This can also be used in a sorting context in hidden surface removal algorithms such as Watkins' algorithm [Roge85] to update which polygon span segments are in front of each other for a given set of scan lines. Other uses of coherence rely on knowledge obtained earlier in the computation to reduce calculations in the generation of the image.

In parallel computing, the approach usually taken for task decomposition is to partition the computation among different processors. This would mean that one could not necessarily rely on values calculated earlier in the computation for later use, as is usually done when exploiting coherence. If coherence is not exploited, redundant calculations are performed and the overall computation time will increase. In order to solve this apparent paradox in a parallel environment, it is worthwhile to investigate possible methods of parallelizing computer graphics display algorithms which maintain coherence. In the taxonomy in section 2.2, the type of coherence which each algorithm exploits in a serial implementation is noted, and we determine the method most suitable for a parallel implementation.

2.1.5. Data Access

One of the key issues in a parallel graphics display algorithm concerns movement of data between memory modules, as well as to and from the disk. Graphics display algorithms use a huge amount of memory, and memory management is important to the overall performance of the algorithm. Remote access of shared data will slow down an algorithm, so data locality should be taken into account when possible. Most algorithms developed in the past were based on simulations rather than implementations on actual multiprocessors, and little attention was placed on data access. In some cases, the given algorithm enforces a certain type of access pattern, but in general, the algorithms can be modified to use any particular type of memory access.

Since datasets representing complex graphics scenes are generally large, it is not feasible to copy the entire dataset onto each node of a multiprocessor. Besides the fact that space may be a limitation, it would not necessarily be desirable to copy all of the data since the time taken to do so on a massively parallel machine would be rather lengthy. Although such a complete replication of data is potentially feasible for read-only data through a one-time broadcast, simple replication cannot be used for read-write data. An example of a read-write data structure in a graphics application is the frame buffer memory used to store the pixel color information. This type of data structure must be partitioned among the memory modules. Of course, one could duplicate this data structure on every processor and perform a parallel merge operation at the end. This would require much more memory for implementation than partitioning the data, in addition to the time required for the merging operation. Shared memory multiprocessors provide a uniform view of the processors' data space, with each memory location being accessible from any processor. In the case of shared memory multiprocessors, the memory latency for data on a non-local memory module is significantly higher than that for a reference to the local memory module. Hence, judicious distribution of data among the memory modules can have a significant impact on realized performance.

2.1.6. Scalability

One issue that has not been dealt with in the past is the ability of the algorithm to provide good speedup on large processor configurations. Some algorithms in the past have been designed with a set multiprocessor configuration in mind, and optimization is limited to this particular size. Due to the rapidly decreasing cost of microprocessors, very large parallel processors will be available in the future. Already, Ncube has a 4096 processor machine and BBN's TC2000 is capable of supporting up to 512 processors using a shared memory paradigm. While these algorithms cannot be tested on such a large machine at the present time, they can be evaluated for their potential performance on massively parallel architectures.

2.2. Taxonomy of Parallel Graphics Decompositions

In this section, a taxonomy is presented of parallel approaches which can be used to partition a parallel graphics rendering algorithm. The usefulness of each of these approaches for MIMD machines is analyzed in an effort to narrow down the choice of algorithms. The criteria for implementation is based on the issues raised in the previous section. The taxonomy includes possible new decompositions that have not yet been developed as well as results obtained by previous researchers. Figure 2.2 illustrates the overall structure of the taxonomy.

In the subsections that follow, different parallel approaches to graphics rendering are reviewed within the structure of the taxonomy. A number of approaches devised in the past were intended as special purpose architectural designs. In some cases, these algorithms could also be used for a multiprocessor and they are discussed here, noting that the original design was for a hardware implementation. Although it would be preferable to include all work that has been done in this subject area, only representative examples of each of the categories in the taxonomy are presented. Other related work is quoted and references are given to provide as complete a listing as possible.

A large contingent of ray tracing algorithms has been developed for parallel implementation. Since this book focuses primarily on fast graphics rendering algorithms, and ray tracing is typically an order of magnitude slower than a conventional tiling algorithm, this approach was analyzed in the tests described here. Some ray tracing designs are still worthy of note due to their unique methods of task partitioning or memory usage, so a selection of these are described in the taxonomy. A paper which provides a good synopsis of parallel approaches to a variety of graphics algorithms is [Burk90].

In the following subsections, brief descriptions of the various algorithms which fit into the various categories of the taxonomy are given.

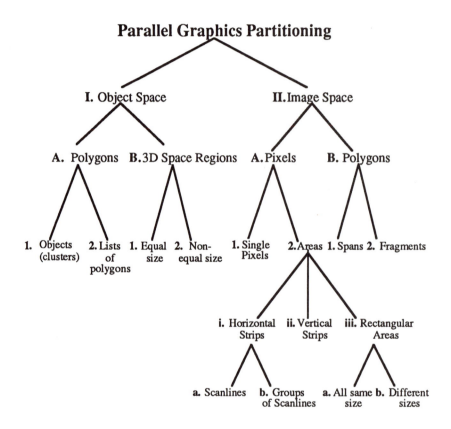

Figure 2.2: Taxonomy of approaches to parallel graphics partitioning

2.2.1. Object Space

Parallel object space decompositions are rare because there has been very little development of object space graphics rendering algorithms. The principal advantage of an object space algorithm is that the hidden surface removal calculation can be computed at arbitrary accuracy. In general, though, the computations in an object space algorithm are inefficient and are more difficult to program in comparison to image space methods. Nevertheless, some researchers have chosen to go this route for a parallel rendering algorithm; these are described next.

2.2.1.1. Polygons

Partitioning tasks based on polygons can be accomplished in a number of different ways: clusters of objects or sub-objects and lists of polygons.

Abram

Abram [Abra86] used Weiler and Atherton's hidden surface removal algorithm, but instead of using their concave polygon clipper, he implemented a fairly simple convex polygon clipper such as the one described by Sutherland [Suth75]. More clipping operations were required than in the concave clipping approach, but the code was simple to implement and did not contain unruly pathological cases such as are present in the Weiler-Atherton clipper. The rest of the algorithm is basically the same as the serial Weiler-Atherton approach, with extensions to facilitate a parallel approach designed for a hardware implementation. As the clipping procedure recursively builds inside and outside lists of polygons based on a clip polygon, a tree structure of lists is created. The tree depends strongly on the input data, but it is built up rather quickly. In Abram's design, the tree is laid out onto a linear pipeline architecture with nodes of the tree mapped to processors in a pipeline. This section of the algorithm only solves the hidden surface removal problem, however. Abram suggests that the tiling problem can then be solved by attaching tiler processors which take the input of visible polygon fragments from the pipeline section and perform the actual illumination and scan conversion of pixels which are then output to a frame buffer. Although Abram's algorithm is specifically tailored as a hardware design, it could easily be mapped to a commercial multiprocessor.

Kankanhalli and Franklin

In a recent paper, Kankanhalli and Franklin [Fran90] present a completely different approach to object space parallelism that deals not only with lists of polygons, but also with edge lists and areas on the screen called *cells*. The algorithm is basically a parallel version of Franklin's [Fran80] object space hidden surface removal algorithm. The algorithm involves constructing a grid which is overlaid on the scene and then determining the covering faces within the grid cells. There are numerous stages of the algorithm, and each stage is a setup to the next stage. Synchronization is required after each stage of the algorithm which can degrade overall performance. This algorithm was implemented on a Sequent Balance with 15 processors, and the hidden surface removal performance was analyzed for two small images. The authors note that the speedup is different for the hidden surface removal section than it is for the visible region reconstruction section. Next, a brief summary and analysis of each of the object space algorithms is presented.

Summary
In the case of Abram's and Kankanhalli's algorithms, the added complexity of the hidden surface removal sections presents a more difficult programming task, in addition to the fact that efficiency in these approaches is not that high. In fact, Kankanhalli calculates a speedup factor of 10 for just the hidden surface removal in his algorithm utilizing 15 processors, resulting in an efficiency of only 0.67. Speedup is a measure of parallel algorithm performance in comparing the time on 1 processor versus the time on P processors (in this case, $P = 15$). Efficiency is speedup divided by P. More detail is presented on these measurements in chapter 4. The speedup for the visible region reconstruction portion of the algorithm is only 6 on 15 processors, which gives an efficiency of only 0.4. Since the total performance of the algorithm is bottlenecked by its slowest part, in addition to the synchronization required between sections, this algorithm does not provide performance which is adequate enough for high performance on large processor configurations.

The tiling section is a separate add-on task to both of these algorithms. Tiling dominates the total display calculation time these days, especially when Phong shading and anti-aliasing are added to the rendering phase. Neither of these researchers has developed an adequate method of solving the tiling problem in parallel because the focus of their work was restricted to the hidden surface removal section. Franklin and Kankanhalli's algorithm is based on functional parallelism in addition to data parallelism. The sections of the algorithm are divided into segments, each of which is applied in parallel to the data. Unfortunately, the synchronization required after each segment limits the potential speedup due to the load imbalance incurred at each synchronization point.

2.2.1.2. 3D Space Regions

Regions of three-dimensional space can be partitioned and assigned as tasks. This method has primarily been used in parallelizing ray tracing, and although none of the methods described here serves as a basis for further analysis, an illustration of the algorithms serves to provide an insight into a unique method for partitioning. Ray tracing may be referred to as an image space algorithm since the hidden surface removal is based on a ray shot through a pixel on the screen; however, the actual intersection and illumination calculations are performed in object space. In this instance, the parallelism is devised from a division of the object space.

Cleary *et al.*

Cleary [Clea83] developed a ray tracing algorithm which involves assigning regions of 3D space to each processor. A processor handles rays as they traverse into its region, and then sends the results in ray packets out to the appropriate neighboring processors as they leave the region. Load balancing is not handled directly; rather, it is assumed that the rays traverse through the different parts of the scene in a random manner such that the processors each have approximately the same amount of work. This assumption is not very accurate and hence can lead to poor performance, especially for large processor configurations. A better approach which provides more direct load balancing for ray tracing is given next.

Badouel *et al.*

Badouel [Bado90] presents three approaches to parallel ray tracing, one of which is called the "ray dataflow" approach and is similar to Cleary's algorithm. The others are described in section 2.2.2 on image space partitioning. Badouel attempts to load balance 3D regions by clustering together equal size smaller regions depending on their expected time complexity. The regions are clustered together so that the clusters themselves have approximately the same time complexity as each other. The initial time complexity of a region is found by shooting a small group of rays within each small region and recording the calculation time of these rays. The clusters are mapped onto processors statically, and rays are passed through the system as in Cleary's algorithm.

The advantage of both of these algorithms is that the database is distributed statically and does not need to be replicated in each processor. Although Badouel's algorithm exhibits better load balancing characteristics than Cleary's approach, this static method of load balancing is not adequate enough for good overall performance.

Caspary and Scherson

Caspary and Scherson [Casp89] developed a ray tracer which is also similar to Cleary's approach for use on a hypercube multiprocessor. A portion of the database is duplicated in each processor, while the bulk of the data is scattered among the processors' memory. By using two processes per processor, load balancing of the work is facilitated. One process handles intersections with the hierarchical database at a high level, while the other one performs intersections between rays and the actual bounding volumes and objects within the local processor. This method handles load balancing, in addition to dealing with memory management effectively.

Challinger

Challinger [Chal91] developed several approaches to parallel volume rendering. The first approach is a parallel extension to object space rendering using the well known *projection* method. The second method is described under the image space processor-per-pixel heading. The parallel implementation of the projection method is an order dependent approach based on which view of the volume cube is seen from the observer's point of view. A visibility graph is constructed which allows one to move voxels into the ready list for parallel rendering. The cells in the ready list can be processed in parallel, but the visibility graph must be updated afterward. This method constitutes a large amount of overhead, but is a unique look into a rendering technique that is quite new.

2.2.1.3. Analysis of Object Space Methods

Object space methods are typically inefficient when compared to image space algorithms. This is especially true of the ray tracing solutions, which is the reason these are not implemented. If the accuracy of the non-ray tracing object space methods is needed for a particular reason (such as to allow changing of the illumination after the hidden surface calculation), then these methods may be worthy of implementation. This is not a concern for most everyday applications, however.

2.2.2. Image Space

Parallel image space partitioning methods are much more prevalent in the literature than the object space methods. They are more suitable for hardware implementation, and there are many adaptations of this type of algorithm. The image space algorithms can be divided into two subsets: those based on pixels or groups of pixels, and those based on polygons or polygon fragments as noted in the taxonomy. An important point to note here is that most of the previous work in this area specifies only how the image is divided up, not how the underlying algorithm is implemented nor how the memory referencing technique is employed. In addition, the algorithms mentioned were simulated rather than implemented on a multiprocessor. The primary reason for this is that very few researchers have had access to such machines until recently. The methods presented here at best only indicate their expected performance since the results have only been theoretically analyzed. The only actual implementations on commercial multiprocessors presented in the literature are those by Theoharis and Roble.

2.2.2.1. Pixels

Parallel display algorithms which are based on pixels are the most popular type of image space decomposition. The principal reason for this is that the pixel calculations are completely independent of one another, so no synchronization is required and the order of task execution is irrelevant. Algorithms which assign a single pixel as a task are typically designed for hardware implementation. This task size is too fine a granularity for implementation on a general purpose MIMD machine since context switching would severely degrade performance. Several of the parallel approaches which use this level of granularity are described next. Another type of pixel decomposition involves tasks which represent areas of adjacent pixels grouped together in one way or another. These methods are described immediately following the discussion of processor-per-pixel decomposition designs.

Processor-per-Pixel Designs

Fuchs *et al.*
Fuchs' [Fuch85] Pixel-Planes 4 system is a good example of a processor-per-pixel hardware architecture. Each pixel contains a small one-bit ALU in addition to a binary tree of one-bit adders designed to efficiently compute the equation $F(x,y) = Ax + By + C$. This equation is used to test for polygon containment as well as calculation of visibility and illumination. Polygons are sent to all processors, and each pixel processor then determines if the polygon covers its area. If the polygon covers a given processor's pixel,

visibility and shading calculations are performed. The system is somewhat inefficient since each processor must check every polygon in the dataset. Fuchs' recent extension to this system called Pixel Planes-5 alleviates some of the inefficiencies in the first system and is described in [Fuch89].

Whitman and Dyer

Whitman and Dyer [Dyer87] developed a vectorized version of a scan line Z-buffer algorithm. This program was designed for an SIMD vector architecture and featured pipelined pixel processing for the shading and visibility calculations. Although the algorithm is too fine-grained for an MIMD architecture, it could serve as a basis for an algorithm which would be suitable for a multiple processor SIMD architecture.

Plunkett and Bailey

Plunkett and Bailey [Plun85] developed a vectorized version of a ray tracing algorithm that processes rays independently. This algorithm is also designed to run on an SIMD pipeline architecture. Rays are placed into a queue, and when the queue fills up, all of the rays are intersected in pipeline fashion. Any new rays generated are attached to the end of the queue for future processing.

Challinger

Challinger [Chal91] has designed a parallel volume rendering approach based on ray tracing. The results seemed to indicate that assigning a pixel per task used significant overhead, while assigning a scan line per processor (as in the processor-per-area approach elaborated upon next), achieved better performance.

Processor-per-Area Designs

Parallel algorithms which work on groups of adjacent pixels represent the widest variety of partitioning methods that have been researched. The different categories in which these algorithms fall include: horizontal strips, vertical strips, and rectangular areas of pixels. Algorithms which are based on horizontal strips can be divided into two sub-categories: those based on single scan lines and those based on contiguous groups of scan lines as tasks. These groups of scan lines as tasks are referred to as *blocks*.

Kaplan and Greenberg

Kaplan and Greenberg [Kapl79] simulated two different hidden surface algorithms and analyzed them according to their usefulness on a parallel architecture. A Watkins' [Roge85] scan line algorithm is subdivided into P groups of s scan lines, where each group forms a different task for a processor. Their design relies on a central control scheduling mechanism, whereby a task is assigned to a processor as it becomes free. The number of groups or the number of regions can be much larger than the actual number of processors available, allowing dynamic load balancing. Shared memory is not a consideration in their simulation; each processor is assumed to have in its local memory all of the information it needs to perform calculations for its portion of the scene.

Another parallel algorithm due to Kaplan and Greenberg is an adaptation of Warnock's [Roge85] algorithm. A static area mesh to the image space and each task is assigned to one region of the mesh. The Warnock algorithm is executed serially within each region. The mesh is applied at both low (16 x 16) and high resolution (32 x 32) to discern the differences in speed. As might be predictable, the finer grain mesh resulted in a more uniform time/area than the coarser mesh. Both the Watkins' and Warnock decompositions are illustrated in figure 2.3.

The authors suggest three considerations which should be taken into account when deriving a parallel implementation of a hidden surface algorithm: *partitionability*, the method of dividing the computation among independent tasks such that communication is kept to a minimum; *coherence*, the reduction of visible surface calculations by basing them on previously obtained results; and *computational efficiency*, the ability of the parallel processor system to schedule tasks. In addition, the authors believe that characteristics such as image area, image complexity, edge complexity, and how the

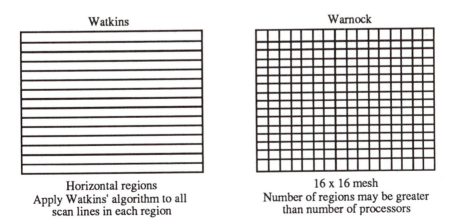

Watkins	Warnock
Horizontal regions	16 x 16 mesh
Apply Watkins' algorithm to all scan lines in each region	Number of regions may be greater than number of processors

Figure 2.3: Two types of decompositions applied by Kaplan and Greenberg

image relates to the algorithm all affect the resultant performance of the algorithms. They also suggest that utilizing a good heuristic task scheduling algorithm is very important in obtaining good load balancing and high performance in the system.

In the Kaplan-Greenberg simulations, a static decomposition approach is applied in dividing up tasks which are then assigned dynamically to processors by the scheduler. Coherence is maintained in a region in their first method (Watkins approach) within scan lines and pixels. In their second method (Warnock approach), area coherence is used within a region of image space. Utilization of the processors is good, especially when the number of regions subdivided is small enough to allow a large number of tasks to be dynamically assigned. Load balancing is also good only when the regions are small enough due to the dynamic task assignment method which is used. As long as the number of regions created is not too large[1], the granularity level of these algorithms is suitable for implementation on a general purpose MIMD machine. The algorithms have good scalability if the number of regions created is adaptable to different processor configurations. The authors state that memory access is local since each processor will contain the data it requires. No clue is given as to how this might be accomplished, though.

Kaplan and Greenberg's algorithms are one of the first efforts in the area of parallel algorithm design for graphics. Their simulations are designed mostly to analyze the difference between two different parallel approaches, not to extrapolate to real world performance. Still, their idea of creating more tasks to achieve better load balancing seems natural. It seems reasonable then to further evaluate their ideas, especially with regard to memory referencing. In any case, this rectangular approach is further investigated in tests described in chapter 5. It is not clear from their paper how many rectangular regions are optimal, nor what type of memory partitioning algorithm should be used. Therefore, the descriptions in chapter 5 include an analysis of methods which can be used to determine these factors.

Chang and Jain

Chang and Jain [Chan81] have simulated a distributed multiprocessor version of Watkins' scan line algorithm. Their idea is to distribute the data among the processors in three-space with either horizontal cross-sections cutting the screen into P horizontal regions or a division of the scene into P cubic regions. This decomposition is shown in figure 2.4. The first method is essentially the same type of

---

[1]This was not quantified by the authors.

decomposition as Kaplan and Greenberg's technique, while the second method divides the areas in a more rectangular fashion. Chang and Jain's algorithm is somewhat different than Kaplan and Greenberg's approach, though, because the polygons are actually clipped in three-space within a single parallel task. Although this might seem to be a 3D decomposition, it is essentially similar to a 2D partition in which the perspective and clipping operations are performed in parallel.

In either of Chang and Jain's decomposition methods, each processor is responsible only for the polygons in its region, allowing parallel data processing. It is not clear from their paper, but one can infer that each processor gets a copy of the entire dataset. This is inefficient since redundant work (in addition to the extra space required) is necessary for the perspective and clipping calculations. Coherence is lost between adjacent regions, and each region has to perform additional three-dimensional clipping, which, as the authors observed, can override the hidden surface calculations if the regions become small enough. The paper considers only a limited number of polygons, and therefore their results cannot be applied to today's imagery. The authors state that due to the independent processing of polygons, each processor must initialize the scan conversion process for its region since there is no coherence between regions. In addition, if polygons are not uniformly distributed among the processors, the resultant time is degraded by the slowest processor. As a possible solution, the authors suggest breaking down the screen according to dataset density so each processor is able to finish close to the same time as the others. This was subsequently implemented by Whelan in his Median-Cut algorithm described later in this chapter.

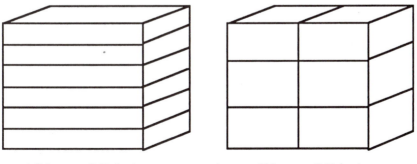

Object space divided up into   Object space divided up into
horizontal cross sections   cubic regions

Figure 2.4: Chang & Jain's decomposition method

Chang and Jain's algorithm is a similar decomposition to Kaplan and Greenberg's method, except that clipping is part of each parallel task as well. The only unfortunate aspect of this is that polygons must be initially stored in all regions (or at least available to all processors) and in the parallel processing phase; the polygons may be clipped multiple times. In most cases, a polygon will not be displayed in a processor's region, but a trivial clip must be done anyway to check for this situation.

Hu and Foley

Hu and Foley [Hu85] analyzed one dynamic and two static distribution methods based on block size variations on a scan line. Their analysis determines to some degree the effect of coherence on parallelism. The static distributions analyzed were denoted the *static contiguous method* and the *static interleave method*. The static contiguous method exploits vertical coherence within a single task, while the static interleave does not. *Static contiguous* refers to a partitioning scheme in which the screen is broken down into P horizontal regions, each containing *y-resolution/P* scan lines. The static interleave method involves partitioning the scan lines among the processors in such a fashion that each processor i would process all scan lines $i, i + P, i + 2*P, i + 3*P$, etc., as is illustrated in figure 2.5.

This technique could have been extended to interleave in the horizontal direction as well, but Hu and Foley chose just to deal with scan

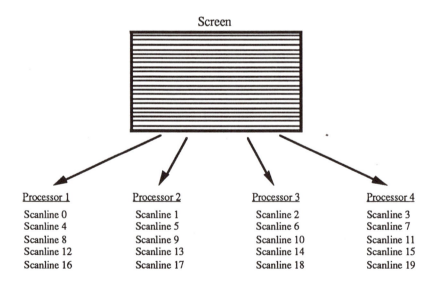

Figure 2.5: Example of scan line to processor assignment in Hu & Foley's interleaving algorithm

lines. The way in which these two static methods attempt to achieve load balancing is different because each tries to minimize different factors. The static contiguous method attempts to capitalize on vertical scan line coherence, a time saving technique used by most sequential algorithms. The downfall of the contiguous method is that it relies on a uniform distribution of the geometric elements in the scene across all blocks of scan lines; an unlikely occurrence. Their interleaving scheme is based on the fact that the geometric elements are not likely to be distributed across scan lines uniformly. Each processor will have nearly equal work since they deal with successive scan lines, but this comes at the expense of vertical scan line coherence. Finally, the *dynamic method* assigns processors to single scan lines in a dynamic scheduling fashion. The dynamic method is similar to Kaplan and Greenberg's idea, except in this case, each task is a single scan line rather than a group of scan lines. The dynamic method follows along the lines of the static interleave approach, except that task to processor assignment is resolved during runtime in the dynamic method, while it is done prior to tiling in the static method.

All static partitioning schemes have one inherent advantage over a dynamic scheme: no scheduling of tasks needs to occur at runtime. In a hardware design which Hu and Foley intended for their algorithm, this can be an important factor. In a software algorithm for a general purpose multiprocessor, this factor is minimized since scheduling must occur for all tasks; therefore, the number of tasks generated is the only overhead. Still, though, the parallel programming method used can have some impact on scheduling overhead. In other words, generating more tasks takes additional time, but this time is small enough to be negligible compared to the running time of a given task (assuming task size is large enough). The main difference between Hu and Foley's dynamic method and their static interleave method is in the task assignment to processors. The dynamic method is implemented (in a simulation on a VAX) at the scan line level by Hu and Foley and obtained the highest performance of the three parallel scan line designs based on their results. Their research involves a simulation of the algorithm on a von Neumann machine since their intention was to build a hardware architecture. Their graphs indicate very good expected performance for the dynamic algorithm when each processor contains the entire dataset. This is not a realistic situation for large databases, so memory storage strategies need to be investigated. If a different memory referencing strategy is implemented, this dynamic technique might provide good speedup and is therefore worth investigating further.

Ghosal and Patnaik

Ghosal and Patnaik present a scan line parallel algorithm that is somewhat similar to Hu and Foley's approach [Ghos86]. They describe several approaches, but their best algorithm is based on processing the scan lines for the y-extent of a single polygon in parallel. Overall parallelism is limited due to the small number of scan lines within the y-extent. In addition, synchronization is necessary after each polygon is finished. Hu and Foley's algorithm seems more general purpose than Ghosal's algorithm, since theirs is not based on the size of the polygon.

Whelan

Whelan [Whel85] compares several different image space task partitioning strategies: a horizontal strip method, a vertical strip method, and a rectangular region method. Whelan's rectangular region method is almost the same as Kaplan and Greenberg's Warnock approach, except that Whelan does not state what serial algorithm is used to tile a single region in his mesh. These methods are simulated to see which exhibits the best overall performance. Although the horizontal and vertical strip schemes might sometimes result in faster times, the rectangular region method is resistant to differences in the imagery and provides the most consistent results. These decomposition methods are illustrated in chapter 5 in figures 5.7, 5.8, and 5.9.

Crockett and Orloff

An algorithm which also uses the horizontal strip method was recently developed by Crockett and Orloff for the Intel iPSC hypercube [Croc91]. This algorithm involves extensive work to take advantage of the message passing architecture of the iPSC/860. Triangles are distributed evenly among the processors, and shading, transforming, and clipping are all performed by the local processor. Each processor is responsible for a region of the frame buffer, so it must receive the triangles from other processors which belong to its area. The processors then take turns passing triangles to the appropriate processor for rasterization, as well as performing the actual rasterization. A conventional Z-buffer is used so that the communication of the triangles can be overlapped with the rasterizing operations. There is a tradeoff between spending time rasterizing triangles and thus not sending out triangles to other processors, and vice versa.

Although the authors present extensive performance analysis for the algorithm and even give a model for the work, they do not focus on the load balancing success of their work decomposition strategy. The bulk of their work seems to be the method by which the communication is done asynchronously within the same processor as the rasterization. This is the primary value of the authors' work since that is a unique problem on this type of machine. In fact, this research could be extended to generalize the data decomposition scheme for any graphics display algorithm on a message passing architecture. Crockett and Orloff also state that the algorithm can be modified for a shared memory architecture. It is clear though, that the modifications given for the latter case represent such a departure from their original design that it should not even be considered the same algorithm.

Parke

Parke [Park80] uses a technique which is based on the traditional Z-buffer. He distributes portions of the image space to processors arranged in a tree structure. Essentially, a hierarchy of regions is created and divided among the processors, with the complexity reduced as the tree is traversed. The output of a parent splitter is the input of the child, and so on, until the content of a region is sent to a single processor. This is illustrated in figure 2.6. Parke uses a Z-buffer which is partitioned among the processors, with each processor handling a portion of the Z-buffer to avoid contention for common memory. This design was intended to be a special purpose machine; however, a simulation is described in Parke's paper.

Parke also describes Fuchs' approach to the problem, in which a central broadcast controller distributes the input data and the Z-

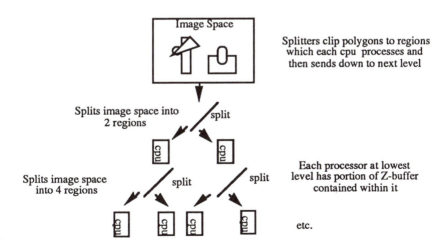

Figure 2.6: Parke's splitter tree of processors

buffer memory is segmented in an interlace fashion rather than a contiguous one as in Parke's original design. A hybrid of the two algorithms is suggested as the best possible alternative since this would alleviate the under-utilization problem.

Parke's initial algorithm is a static decomposition and relies on a uniform distribution of objects in the scene, so each processor will be just as busy as its neighbors. Assuming Parke's hybrid algorithm could be implemented, load balancing and utilization might be optimized. Communication can become a bottleneck in his system due to the passing of polygons from level to level in the tree. The algorithm is a standard Z-buffer algorithm, which means it suffers from the aliasing problem that is inherent in that methodology. It could be extended to be solved with any of the anti-aliasing methods common today, however. The principal limitations of the algorithm are the large amount of communication and the lack of adequate load balancing. This makes Parke's method unsuitable for implementation on a general purpose multiprocessor machine.

Theoharis

One unusual parallel implementation of a hidden surface algorithm is by Theoharis [Theo86] for use on a network of Inmos Transputers. Theoharis' method uses a variation of Parke's splitter mechanism. This algorithm assigns portions of the computer graphics display pipeline to different processors, and passes the information from one processor to the next until a scan conversion processor handles the actual rendering section. Each transputer handles a polygon and performs clipping, hidden surface elimination, and scan conversion in a pipeline format. The transputer has very fast context switching between processes, which makes it ideal to support fast changes as polygons come down the pipe. Clipping is performed via the Sutherland-Hodgman (see [Roge85]) polygon clipping algorithm, with each clipping plane forming a stage of the pipe. Then, multiple scan converters run in parallel, accepting polygons and generating pixel lists of those pixels covered by that polygon. A buffer routine forms the last stage of the pipe, which runs a standard Z-buffer hidden surface removal algorithm for the allocated image partition. Once all pixels have been handled, the frame buffer is displayed. Parke's splitter mechanism is employed to further limit the number of polygons handled. The algorithm is illustrated in figure 2.7. The pipeline does not consist of that many stages, so it needs to be expanded out in a tree fashion (steps 8 & 9 in the figure). The splitter mechanism accomplishes this by creating a tree of processes running in parallel which can form their own pipes and keep the available processors busy.

Theoharis' scheme has the disadvantage that he assumes as Parke did that the image is uniformly distributed between all of the split planes. If this is not the case, some processors will have less work to do than others. He mentions that this problem can be alleviated by random splitting of non-contiguous areas in order to achieve load balancing, but this has not been investigated. Theoharis' algorithm uses a functional parallel decomposition, and it is possible that the communication between processors might limit the speed of the program. Processors performing the clipping and transformations will almost certainly be faster than the processors performing the scan conversion, leading to a bottleneck in the system. In this case, the load will not be universally balanced among all of the processors. In addition, some processors might be assigned sections of the scene which are far less complex than other sections. Although the algorithm illustrates a novel approach to the problem of a parallel hidden surface method, the solution given may not be able to be applied to a general purpose multiprocessor which does not have the communication properties of the Transputer. The real limitations in the algorithm are the assumed uniformity in the image and the large amount of communication, which are the same problems from which Parke's algorithm suffers. These algorithms might be suitable for hardware implementation, but are not appropriate for use on a conventional multiprocessor.

Whitman

The author of this book previously developed a parallel version of an area coherence scheme similar to Warnock's method [Warn69]; it

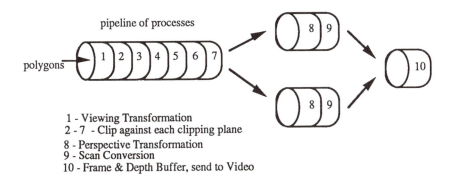

1 - Viewing Transformation
2 - 7 - Clip against each clipping plane
8 - Perspective Transformation
9 - Scan Conversion
10 - Frame & Depth Buffer, send to Video

Figure 2.7: Theoharis' pipeline of processes for image decomposition

is illustrated in figure 2.8. This methodology employs a dynamic decomposition whereby a region is subdivided if it is too complex to compute. Instead of being recursive as in Warnock's original design, the algorithm assigns the subdivisions to separate processors, and the same tests are performed again within these subdivisions. If the region is too complex again, more subdivisions are created. Processes are assigned to subdivisions, and as a processor becomes free, it is assigned to a region. Coherence is maintained via the area method, which can be taken down to the pixel level if necessary.

There are several problems with this implementation of the Warnock algorithm in parallel. This algorithm is excellent for hidden line removal, but if it is used for hidden surface removal, the algorithm is not well suited for tiling polygons. One method would involve tiling each region at the point of hidden surface removal, but this creates a huge number of tasks. In addition, edge lists and other data structures need to be built for each small region, involving a lot of overhead. If the approach suggested in Warnock's paper is used, the tiling would be a separate operation. Synchronization needs to occur prior to tiling, and then a visible region reconstruction algorithm similar to that of Kankanhalli needs to be performed. This extra synchronization degrades performance, in addition to the fact that another entirely separate technique is required for tiling the visible regions in parallel.

The granularity of tasks created using the Warnock method is too fine for a general purpose parallel machine. The high context switching creates too much overhead in this approach since there are so many tasks created and the execution time of each task is very

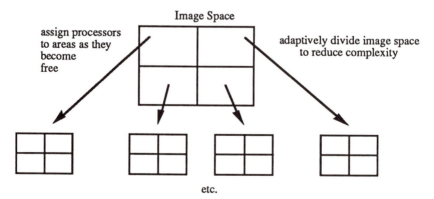

Figure 2.8: Whitman's parallel variation on the Warnock subdivision algorithm

small. As a result, the performance of the algorithm in parallel is not
very good. Secondly, while the Warnock algorithm is adequate for
hidden line removal, it is fairly slow compared to other image space
algorithms for hidden surface removal. For very large polygons it
might provide reasonable results, but the datasets which are typical
in today's imagery are large, meaning that the average polygon size is
smaller than when Warnock developed his algorithm. These two
factors indicate that this algorithm is not a good choice for implementation.

Painter's Algorithm

The painter's algorithm due to Newell, Newell, and Sancha
[Roge85] might make an interesting candidate for a parallel
algorithm. The problem with converting the painter's algorithm to a
parallel environment is the requirement for a specified order of tiling
the polygons. This might be alleviated if regions could be specified as
tasks and the painter's algorithm could work as a serial approach
within each task. In fact, any hidden surface algorithm could be
implemented as a serial task within any of the area based approaches
because they do not rely on a functional decomposition. This is
because of the independent nature of these tasks.

A generalized implementation of the Newell, Newell, and Sancha
algorithm in parallel has not been presented in the literature, and it
is easy to see why. The synchronization necessary to make sure that
pixels are not overwritten in incorrect order will limit the potential
speedup of the algorithm.

Adaptive Algorithms

While the methods described to this point all involve decompositions
without regard to the data input set, several approaches have been
developed that attempt to take into account the input scene when
partitioning the work. These schemes are outlined next and take into
account the work in a given area of the screen to estimate a priori
how to divide the work among the processors. Whelan uses the
centroids of polygons as their locations, and attempts to assign an
equal number of polygons to each processor. Roble similarly tries to
assign an equal number of polygons per processor, but he uses a
bounding box and the regions are determined differently.

Whelan

Whelan [Whel85] is one of the first researchers to suggest a
scheme based on non-equal size areas. This method (which is distinct
from his other approaches) is called the *Median Cut* algorithm and
proceeds as follows. The idea behind the algorithm is the creation of a

median line across a given region, in which half of the polygons are in one sub-region and half in the other sub-region. To achieve this, the image space is divided recursively, based on the centroids of the data elements. At each recursion level, the median of the centroids of all polygons in the region is used as a dividing line, alternately in the horizontal and vertical directions. This process of subdividing is repeated until the number of subdivisions equals the number of processors. Although it is not an optimal partitioning scheme, it can produce very favorable results on a variety of data input sets. The unfortunate drawback is that determining the location of the partitions involves sorting the centroids many times, and this overhead is hard to overcome in the performance of the rest of the algorithm.

Whelan's results indicate that his Median Cut algorithm has the potential for high performance, but it exhibits a significant amount of start-up overhead. Since this approach was not deemed viable by Whelan, his rectangular area approach, which is a generalization of Kaplan and Greenberg's parallel Warnock method, holds the most promise. This latter method could be adapted to any number of processors and still have a minimum overhead.

Roble

Roble [Robl88] has developed a scan line Z-buffer algorithm which is designed to exploit load balancing prior to the tiling stage. It is similar to Kaplan and Greenberg's area approach and was implemented on the Intel iPSC hypercube. Roble's idea involves counting the number of polygons sent to each processor under a given partition. If there is a strong discrepancy between the processors as to the number of polygons handled, the cube manager re-partitions the scene again so a nearly uniform distribution is achieved. This is a fairly dynamic solution since the tasks are updated during runtime. It is essentially the same as Badouel's clustering technique described in section 2.2.1.2, except that no prior work is required since the number of polygons is used as a heuristic to indicate the amount of work in a region. The decomposition is based on the input polygons, and load balancing is partially solved with this method. Memory contention is not an issue since once tasks are divided, each processor independently solves the hidden surface problem. This is a good solution for a multiprocessor with a small (< 50 or so) number of processors, but as the number of processors is scaled up, the region size is smaller and there will be more overhead.

Roble divides the screen space into P equal sections and passes polygons to the processors for each section. If the number of polygons in certain sections creates a situation where some nodes have more work to do than others, the sections are merged and divided in an attempt to create an equal computational load for each processor. This type of approach is just a variation on the rectangular region decomposition theme, except that the region sizes are different depending on the amount of work present. Roble had some success with this approach, and Whelan showed his Median Cut algorithm to provide the best overall solution among his comparisons. Both authors state that the overhead can be quite costly and can override any performance gains. It seems worthwhile that if the overhead can be limited, then this type of algorithm will provide good performance in an implementation.

Analysis of Algorithms for Pixel Decomposition

It seems clear that the processor-per-pixel architectures and algorithms involve a very fine grain solution which is not applicable to implementation on this type of machine. The primary reason is that the task size is too small and context switching would dominate the computation. On the other hand, the processor-per-area designs are better suited to implementation on a general purpose multiprocessor. This is because the task size in these designs is large enough to eliminate context switching problems, yet it can be varied to handle load balancing in a variety of ways.

Other algorithms seek to distribute data to processors in a static manner so that no further communication takes place between the processors. After the graphics space is divided up, the hidden surface removal and rendering calculations are performed within a single processor for each section. Chang and Jain use this approach by statically dividing up three-space and assigning P processors to P regions. The disadvantage of this approach is that good load balancing is not achieved since uniformity of the image is not a realistic scenario. Whelan and Roble attempt to directly solve this by using a static decomposition which determines to some degree the amount of work assigned to each processor.

2.2.2.2. Polygons

Z-buffer
One of the more interesting sequential graphics display algorithms is the Z-buffer due to Catmull [Catm74]. This algorithm could be modified to process individual polygons as tasks. A parallel version of the Z-buffer might work as follows. A full screen Z-buffer memory is stored in globally shared memory and scattered

throughout the system. Each processor scan-converts a single polygon as a task and writes the pixel value into the scattered frame buffer if the value of the Z-buffer is greater than the z-value of the polygon at that pixel. To handle anti-aliasing, a very large Z-buffer and frame buffer could be used and post-filtered down to the desired output resolution. Although Parke and Theoharis ultimately use a Z-buffer, their decompositions are screen space subdivisions, although Theoharis' has features of both. This method involves parallelism by polygon with a shared Z-buffer.

The parallel Z-buffer algorithm suffers from the problem of contention for a shared resource. This method would require constant referencing of the Z-buffer array, and collisions in remote memory access would likely occur, slowing down the algorithm tremendously. This solution might be adequate for small processor configurations, but would not be suitable for a large MIMD machine.

Allison

A slightly different version of a Z-buffer algorithm which has been implemented on the BBN Butterfly TC2000 is due to Allison [Alli91]. His algorithm involves a parallel decomposition in which each object is sent to a different processor for scan-conversion. The limitation of this approach is that the algorithm is limited in its parallelism by the number of objects in the scene. For scientific datasets, this may not be that bad since most scientific programs use hundreds if not thousands of objects. Another problem, as noted above, is the contention for the shared Z-buffer. Synchronization is accomplished by a lock on each pixel. Objects which cover a large portion of the screen tend to slow the algorithm down, presumably because of blocking of pixel access for other objects. This algorithm is an initial stab at using the TC2000 for parallel processing of graphics rendering. The only problem is that the success of the algorithm depends to a large extent on the composition of the scene.

Fiume, Fournier, and Rudolph

Fiume, Fournier, and Rudolph [Fium83] simulated a version of a spanning scan line algorithm for an ultracomputer, which would be similar in design to the NYU Ultracomputer. The processors use the Fetch and Add instruction (called RepAdd in the paper) to assure atomic access to write operations in shared memory. They also propose an addition, the RepMin operation, which would write and replace the element in shared memory if the new one is less than it. This could be used to perform the hidden surface elimination. The polygons are broken down into span-areas which are related to vertices rather than scan lines. Each span-area is a trapezoidal or triangular region, and each processing element (*PE*) processes the different areas in parallel. All PEs synchronize at the end of processing for each scan line. The authors claim that this is not necessary, and if sufficient memory is available, the technique could be generalized to k scan lines, $k \geq 1$. An example distribution of PEs is illustrated in figure 2.9.

One problem mentioned in the paper is that all PEs could be waiting for a single PE to finish calculation on a long span. The authors suggest subdividing a span if it is larger than some M maximum number of pixels. In order to incorporate anti-aliasing into the algorithm, a coverage mask (8 x 8) is used for the span-area covering a pixel. The weight (mask) of a particular span-area is the fraction of the area of the pixel covered corresponding to the number of one bits assigned to the span-area. Anti-aliasing is calculated after a PE has computed the hidden surface calculations for its pixels on the scan line. The authors' goals were to achieve performance which was better than a sequential algorithm, as well as a parallel method for computing anti-aliasing.

The Fiume *et al.* algorithm suffers from a few limitations. First, the fact that the processors need to synchronize at the end of a scan line forces the algorithm to slow down to the speed of the slowest processor, and this is done at every scan line. It is not clear whether one could take advantage of multiple scan line parallel processing, as

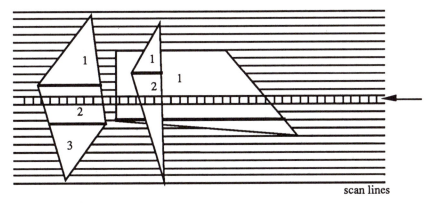

scan lines

For marked scan line, a PE handles span-area 2 in first polygon, a PE handles span-area 1 in second polygon, and a PE handles span-area 2 in overlapping third polygon. Anti-aliasing and display is synchronized at end of scan line.

Figure 2.9: Trapezoidal span areas each processed by a separate PE per scan line

suggested by the authors in their paper, to solve this problem. The reason is that it may be difficult to synchronize processing of the same span-areas from scan line to scan line. The decomposition is a dynamic approach, but is limited by the synchronization problem. Scan line as well as pixel coherence is exploited. Since the ultracomputer architecture seems to have fast context switching, the utilization of each processor is very good.

Load balancing is a difficult issue, since some processors may be busy with large spans while others are processing short spans, even with span subdivision. Scalability can be solved, but only if there are more spans on the scan line to accommodate the additional processors. The algorithm was not implemented on an actual multiprocessor, so one cannot tell whether a large number of processors would produce a good speedup. It seems that since the parallelism is assigned to PEs by span areas (S) and if $S < P$, some processors will go underutilized. This seems to be one of the major limitations of the algorithm. Memory referencing is not as important an issue, especially with the fetch and add instruction. The constructs are somewhat different than in other multiprocessors, but are not hard to program.

2.2.3. Summary

Based on the algorithms analyzed here, it seems logical that the choice of an image space parallel algorithm based on rectangular areas of pixels holds the most promise for high performance. Note that the work decomposition strategy only amounts to a small portion of the total parallel algorithm. The setup overhead prior to rendering, in addition to the memory referencing strategy, represents an additional issue that affect the overall performance. The implementations analyzed in the remainder of this book are given next.

1. A scan line algorithm similar to the one introduced by Hu and Foley. The dynamic assignment method shown by Hu and Foley indicates a potential for good performance even with the loss of vertical coherence. Since this algorithm was simulated and not implemented, a multiprocessor implementation of this algorithm is necessary to refute or substantiate their claims. In addition, the database storage issue was not fully addressed in their research.

2. A rectangular region algorithm such as the one suggested by Kaplan and Greenberg as well as the one by Whelan. This

method seems to be the most logical choice for parallel implementation since the granularity of tasks can be varied. Although Kaplan and Greenberg determined that a finer granularity yielded better performance, they did not analyze this to any degree. Neither of these research efforts fully addressed the memory storage and access issue, and their results are based on simulations rather than real-world implementations, so a full analysis is necessary.

3. An algorithm which uses a type of task assignment similar to the static approach suggested by Whelan's Median Cut algorithm. Whelan showed that this method resulted in the best performance of all of his simulated algorithms. The problem was that the overhead necessary to determine the task decomposition prior to tiling degraded the overall performance. A simpler type of static approach which is not as accurate as the Median Cut algorithm might perform nearly as well, but without the substantial overhead.

4. A task decomposition scheme which is similar to the rectangular region algorithm involving task sizes determined at runtime. This is based on an idea by Rao and Kumar [Rao89] in which tasks are dynamically split during parallel execution. This approach to load balancing would seem to be a good extension to the rectangular region method.

While some algorithms listed here have been developed in the past, they have not been thoroughly analyzed in terms of task partitioning and memory referencing schemes. In particular, previous efforts by other researchers have not addressed a number of issues relating to computer graphics and parallel processing. These previous efforts have largely been attempts at obtaining parallel graphics display solutions without a thorough analysis of the problem. Some of the issues not addressed in full include:

- Mapping of algorithm to intended architecture
- Size and distribution of tasks
- Memory distribution and communication
- Coherence and parallelism
- Load balancing

The preceding items are fully analyzed in the designs presented in chapter 5. Since the algorithms are implemented on a particular machine rather than simulated, it is also possible to determine quantitatively how well each implementation has succeeded.

2.3. Conclusions

In the first section of this chapter, a number of criteria are given to evaluate the different parallel decompositions which are presented in the second section. These criteria for evaluation include granularity, type of parallelism, use of coherence, load balancing characteristics, methods of data access, and scalability.

In the second section, a number of past as well as yet untested possible parallel approaches are presented and categorized into a taxonomy. The image space pixel decompositions based on areas of pixels seem to hold the most promise for high performance on an MIMD architecture. In chapter 5, the implementations of approaches are described in an effort to conclusively show that one technique is optimal. Since most of the past work has involved simulations and not multiprocessor implementations, these implementations allow us to compare different task decompositions and memory referencing strategies on an equal basis for the first time.

3

Issues in Parallel Algorithm Development

In this chapter, different advanced parallel computer architectures are compared according to their suitability for implementation of a graphics display algorithm.

In the first section, the architectures are presented and analyzed with regard to the development of a parallel graphics rendering algorithm. Although SIMD architectures (single instruction, multiple data path) have been used for graphics applications in the past, this mode of operation generally requires task execution in lock step fashion. Work done at the pixel level can be accomplished in this manner, but higher level tasks are not well suited to this type of parallel approach.

The type of architectures investigated here is restricted to MIMD machines (multiple instruction, multiple data path) since different tasks can proceed simultaneously under separate control flow. These machines can be configured with small to large processor counts, allowing flexibility in performance versus cost. An inexpensive MIMD architecture can be obtained for as little as $10,000, while extremely high performance machines can cost several million dollars. The algorithms presented here are designed to be useful on a small system containing only 2 processors, as well as a large system of 100 or more processors.

The second section involves a comparison of the two main architectural choices in MIMD hardware. These two methods, message passing and shared memory, are analyzed with regard to a parallel graphics implementation. Finally, we describe the programming environment which is specific to the BBN Butterfly multiprocessor since this machine was chosen for the implementation comparisons here.

3.1. Architectural Choices

There are currently a number of commercial message passing architectures (Intel iPSC, NCube, Inmos transputer based machines) and shared memory multiprocessors (Sequent Balance, Encore Multimax, Alliant FX/2800, and BBN Butterfly[1]) on the market. Coarse grained MIMD architectures such as those offered by Cray, Convex, Silicon Graphics, and others allow only limited parallelism. The issues in developing programs for the latter machines are not as pronounced as for the previously mentioned machines due to their small processor counts (typically 2 to 8 processors).

In this section, we describe a few specific commercial machines to illustrate the differences among the classes of architectures. These differences allow us to evaluate how well the various types of computer image generation algorithms can be expected to run on a variety of parallel computers.

The first subsection describes the impact of using conventional MIMD hardware to perform computer graphics rendering. Different issues by which the architectures are evaluated are given in this section. The amount of memory used in a graphics application, as well as the high data movement involved in this application, influences the choice for the appropriate architecture suitable for this type of application.

Distributed memory architectures are useful for applications where the data can be partitioned initially among the nodes[2] of the system with little communication thereafter. These types of machines typically have a high message passing cost, and any time spent

---

[1]BBN Advanced Computers, Inc. is no longer marketing the Butterfly, although it is still being supported.

[2]The terms *processors* and *nodes* are used interchangeably here.

communicating is time wasted from computation. The Intel hypercube family of machines are examples of distributed memory architectures in which the processors are connected in a hypercube topology. Although hypercube connections are a common design, Intel is also experimenting with a mesh design on what is currently reported to be the fastest computer in the world: the prototype Intel Touchstone machine installed at California Institute of Technology.

The BBN Butterfly contains physically distributed memory, but it is classified as a shared memory architecture since remote memory can be logically shared. The Encore Multimax is an example of global shared memory architecture which uses caching to speed up references to the memory modules. These machines are analyzed as representative examples of their genre in the second subsection.

3.1.1. Impact of Graphics Rendering on System Requirements

Utilizing a multiprocessor for an application such as computer graphics rendering imposes certain demands on the system that other applications might not introduce. The large amount of data movement in this type of algorithm presents unusual problems for certain types of architectures. Following are two characteristics of graphics display algorithms which can affect the performance of the computer architecture to be used for implementation of the software algorithm.

3.1.1.1. Image Quality

In this book, we are primarily interested in trying to achieve good performance when rendering highly complex images in a graphics display algorithm on a parallel processor. This increase in image complexity can arise from several factors given in [Whit89]:

Anti-aliasing. This is a correction mechanism for the typically inadequate sampling of high frequencies in a computer generated scene. More information about the geometric structure of the scene must be available to do anti-aliasing, and this affects the size of the data structures and the amount of information which must be shared by each processor. In general, polygon fragment or sub-pixel information must be stored to perform anti-aliasing.

Mapping. The data structures required for texture, bump, and reflection mapping are very large and must be shared by a large number of processors, which increases the communication between processors. These mapping operations enhance the quality of the image by simulating different types of surface attributes for the objects in the scene.

Shadows. Some shadow casting algorithms require data structures as large as those required for texture, bump, and reflection mapping, with the same resultant communication problems. If a Z-buffer shadow algorithm is used, the visibility calculations are repeated for each light source and this adds time complexity [Will78]. The shadow volumes technique requires additional geometric data and this adds to the memory requirement [Crow77].

Resolution. Instead of generating 640 x 484[3] images, 1280 x 968 or evengreater pixel resolution is desired to enhance image quality.

Data Elements. An increase in the number of geometric elements provides enhanced realism in the scene.

Anti-aliasing, mapping, and shadowing involve increasing the complexity of the rendering calculations. Increased resolution raises the number of rendering calculations necessary since more pixels are displayed. Shadow casting and higher resolution increase the overall realism in the scene description by providing more detail. Each factor which increases image quality introduces distinct problems into the parallelization process. The random access memory referencing patterns associated with mapping and shadow casting can degrade performance significantly if this data is not managed effectively. The implementation of these factors in a parallel environment is strongly dependent on the decomposition and general memory referencing scheme chosen. Because this book focuses primarily on the analysis of the decomposition and memory referencing strategies, the focus here is on anti-aliasing, resolution, and number of data elements, leaving mapping and shadowing to be analyzed in a future work. Both greater resolution in image size and larger datasets require more memory to be available in the system.

If the frame buffer is stored internally in RAM and resolution is increased from 640 x 484 to 1280 x 968, the memory storage requirements quadruple. If a Z-buffer [Catm74] or A buffer [Carp84] hidden

---

[3]This refers to a display resolution of 640 pixels across by 484 pixels down the screen, which is standard video resolution.

surface algorithm is used, even more memory is needed due to the additional data stored per pixel. For a 1280 x 968 image maintaining 4 bytes for red, green, blue, and coverage in addition to 4 bytes for the z-value, 8 megabytes of memory is needed. This memory needs to be accessible by all of the processors.

An increase in the number of geometric elements also requires a corresponding linear increase in the memory required. If we assume that the elements used are quadrilateral polygons, each polygon requires 12 bytes to store each point, 12 bytes to store each normal, and 10 bytes (minimally) to store the connectivity information. This adds up to 106 bytes per polygon, although we can in general assume that each normal and point are shared by 4 other polygons. This results in 32 bytes per polygon. Based on these values, the amount of memory can be determined for different levels of image quality, as shown next.

The following are scenarios for memory usage based on image quality. Memory requirements for each image quality level are variable within a certain range, depending on the features included and the algorithm chosen.

> Case 1. A "low quality" image generated today might involve 1,000 to 10,000 geometric elements at a resolution of 640 x 484 (standard video resolution).
> Memory requirement for data: 32K up to 320K
> Case 2. A "normal" image would involve 10,000 to 70,000 geometric elements, include at least anti-aliasing and possibly additional visual effects. Resolution would be 640 x 484 up to 1280 x 968.
> Memory requirement for data: 320K up to 2.2 megabytes
> Case 3. A "high quality" image would involve 70,000 up to 1,000,000 geometric elements, include anti-aliasing and one or more visual effects. Resolution would be 1280 x 968 up to 4K x 4K.
> Memory requirement for data: 2.2 megabytes up to 32 megabytes

These estimates do not include storage for maintaining edgelists and interpolation values, in addition to the space required for advanced features such as anti-aliasing. Frame buffer or Z-buffer storage in RAM will make matters worse at all levels. The actual memory requirements are at least double and possibly quadruple the values given previously for the data storage. Access to all of this data remotely on a shared memory machine will likely cause problems with excessive usage of the interconnection network unless the data is carefully managed. On message passing architectures, access to remote data requires knowledge of the location of the data and a complex mechanism for distributing it among the processors in the system. In addition, the time to pass the data back and forth in a message passing machine will degrade performance. One of the reasons to use a multiprocessor for graphics rendering is to handle large and complicated scenes. Therefore, the memory requirements and manipulation of data in the system need to be carefully evaluated to reduce the overhead effects.

3.1.1.2. I/O

Some advanced architectures use parallel disk setups such as the data vault mechanism in the Connection Machine. In general, though, most multiprocessors employ only a single disk for I/O. The large scene descriptions required in various applications may require a time of several seconds up to many minutes to read in the data from disk. This can only be accomplished sequentially on a conventional von Neumann architecture. In a parallel machine, however, this presents a bottleneck in performance if only one processor interacts with the disk. One can see that it is desirable to be able to exploit some type of parallelism in disk usage. At the end of the graphics computation, an image is sent out either to an external frame buffer or to the disk for storage. This operation should also be parallelized. The assumption in this book is that only a single disk is available for I/O operations, so parallelism may take the form of pipelining. For machines which allow parallel I/O, performance will greatly benefit if this feature is exploited.

As was stated in chapter 1, the I/O phases of a display algorithm are not the focus of this book. Too often, though, computer graphics specialists have ignored this portion of the program in their parallel algorithms. The I/O can directly affect how the algorithm is structured and optimization might not be feasible within the context of any given parallel tiling algorithm. An example parallel implementation of the I/O operations is illustrated later in this text.

3.1.2. Message Passing

In a message passing architecture, all of the processors are connected by an interconnection network through which messages are passed. This is the only form of communication between processors because they do not share any memory. The Intel iPSC is an example of this type of architecture. The processor nodes in the iPSC are connected in a hypercube fashion whereby each processor can communicate with n other nodes which differ by exactly one bit in their addresses in a fully configured system containing 2^n nodes. The more recent versions of the Intel hypercube use a type of message passing mechanism that is called "wormhole" routing [Nuge88]. This routing mechanism allows processors to communicate with each other directly even if they are not directly connected. A path which is held open for the entire length of the message is created from the source to the destination. This type of path is only created for sufficiently long messages to prevent unfair use of the interconnection network.

The programmer's burden of "mapping" a parallel algorithm onto the hypercube is lessened since optimizing the algorithm for nearest neighbor communication is no longer a necessary consideration for this architecture. The issue of multiple messages contesting for portions of the same path still exists in this scheme since the wormhole is maintained as long as a message is being transferred. If another route is not available, any other messages vying for a portion of this path must wait. In addition to the above hypercube connections between nodes, there exists another processing node called the *cube manager* which is connected to all the processors via ethernet link. A three-dimensional hypercube is illustrated in figure 3.1.

Some choices for algorithm decomposition favor one type of architecture over another solely because of the method of memory distribution. Much work has been directed at the problem of mapping

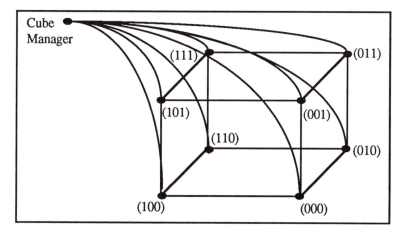

Figure 3.1: Example of hypercube architecture (8 nodes)

algorithms to architectures [Berm87], but no single methodology is optimal across different architectural models and algorithmic paradigms. Since the optimal mapping problem is NP-complete in most realistic settings [Chen88], heuristics are usually used. Sadayappan and Ercal [Sada87] have developed a technique in which data locality is exploited by a nearest neighbor mapping to reduce communication costs in a mesh architecture. This approach would be applicable to a graphics display application when it is to be implemented on such a machine.

The Intel hypercube has several limitations which make this machine a less likely candidate for a graphics image generation implementation. This type of architecture is primarily intended for problems which exhibit high parallelism and high computation costs, but little data movement. The cost of sending messages between the cube manager and each processor, as well as between the processors themselves, is very high and is only reduced when a wormhole is used. A message must contain greater than 256 bytes in order for wormhole routing to occur. The low bandwidth of the ethernet and high set-up time for messages allow only limited dynamic load balancing to be accomplished since data movement is costly. For a graphics display algorithm, the cost of propagating part or all of the database to the nodes is high, as is the cost for retrieving the rendered pixels. Parallel I/O cannot be achieved in this machine since only the cube manager processor can access the disk. The Intel hypercube was not designed for high data movement applications, and therefore the bottleneck created by the cube manager for disk I/O, as well as the cost of message passing, limits the use of this machine for graphics algorithms.

A reasonable solution might involve an initial communication of data to be scattered throughout the processors with successive communication involving very small amounts of data. This would be viable in a graphics context in which the computing cost overwhelmingly outweighs the communication cost, such as in a ray tracing program. Badouel [Bado90] has used a ray tracing algorithm with good success on the iPSC by employing a caching scheme for subsequent communication after the initial data distribution.

3.1.3. Shared Memory

There are a number of distinct interconnection network strategies for connecting processors to a global memory. Next we describe two types of shared memory multiprocessor architectures: bus-based tightly coupled shared memory and multistage switch-based shared memory.

3.1.3.1. Bus-based Shared Memory

The shared memory paradigm allows the programmer to think in terms of parallel tasks, rather than assigning tasks to processors as in a message passing design. The Encore Multimax is an example of a shared memory multiprocessor which uses a single bus for processor to memory communication. Other bus-based systems may use multiple buses for faster communication and fewer conflicts. The Multimax can contain up to 20 processors and from 32 to 128 megabytes of memory. A drawing of this type of architecture is given in figure 3.2, where P indicates a processor.

The Encore's primary limitation is the fixed bandwidth of the bus, which restricts the number of processors that can be used efficiently. This does not allow testing of the algorithm on large scale processor configurations. Another factor weighing against this type of architecture is the notion of a single contiguous memory shared by all processors. Processors do not have any local memory to access, and therefore contention for the bus can become a performance degradation factor even when referencing data that does not need to be shared. A memory cache provides a form of local access and alleviates this bottleneck somewhat. For some algorithmic choices and for initial implementation and debugging, bus-based architectures could be a good choice for a graphics image generation algorithm, but they do not provide the scalable performance that is necessary to achieve fast processing of large graphics databases.

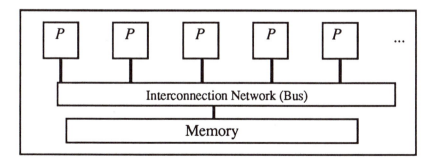

Figure 3.2: An example of a bus-based multiprocessor architecture

3.1.3.2. Switch-based Shared Memory

The BBN family of multiprocessors (which includes the Butterfly GP1000 and TC2000) are shared memory multiprocessors which utilize a complex interconnection network to connect processors to shared memory modules. For the purposes of this discussion, we will restrict ourselves to analyzing the architecture of the Butterfly GP1000. The Butterfly GP1000 is a scalable multiprocessor which can be configured from 1 to 256 processors, each containing 4 megabytes of memory. The network in this machine is built up from a basic 4 x 4 crossbar switch, which allows simultaneous communication between processors and memory as long as more than one processor does not try to communicate with the same memory module at the same time. This switch is shown in figure 3.3. A description of the advantages of this type of switch over a bus-based interconnection network is given in [BBN84].

The memory in this machine can be logically shared, but it is physically distributed across a multi-stage network switch. The processors each have access to their own local memory, as well as to remote memory modules, by making references across the switch. This puts the Butterfly into the NUMA (non-uniform memory access) class of shared memory multiprocessors since the local data access is faster than the remote data access. Other NUMA machines include the Cedar [Kuck86] project from University of Illinois as well as the NYU Ultracomputer [Gott83]. The software interface provided for the programmer in the Butterfly makes this remote referencing transparent. The interconnection network provides very high performance with a 32 Megabit/second communication bandwidth. This network is illustrated in figure 3.4.

There is no notion of a single main processor in the Butterfly, although one of the processors is connected to the multibus and serves as the processor through which I/O is accomplished. This could create a possible I/O bottleneck similar to the one stated previously for the Intel iPSC. In the case of the Butterfly, however, each processor can access the disk transparently through the I/O processor, whereas the cube manager is the only processor which can access the disk in the iPSC. This transparent disk access allows any processor to perform a disk read or write operation, although semaphores may be required to prevent interference. The I/O bottleneck still exists in the GP1000, but it is easier to program the reading in of data in the GP1000 than in the iPSC.

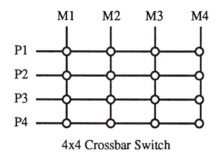

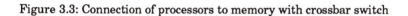

4x4 Crossbar Switch

Figure 3.3: Connection of processors to memory with crossbar switch

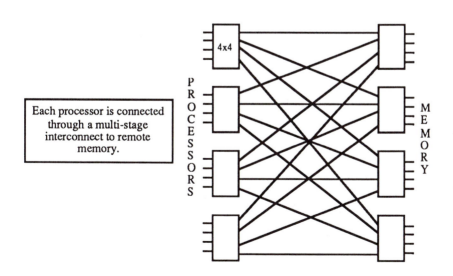

Each processor is connected through a multi-stage interconnect to remote memory.

Figure 3.4: Multi-stage interconnection network in BBN Butterfly

3.2. Comparison of MIMD Methodologies

In comparing shared memory and message passing architectures for a graphics display algorithm, several items are worth considering. One important item to note when choosing an architecture for implementation is the fact that the amount of memory to be managed when generating high quality imagery can grow to be very large. Based on the algorithmic requirements given previously, it is desirable to develop parallel graphics algorithms on a machine with the following characteristics:

1. Ease of programming
2. High performance interconnection network
3. Scalable to high processor configurations

First, the shared memory programming paradigm is generally considered to be easier than message passing for the programmer to work with in developing code for an MIMD computer. The reason is that data which all processors need access to can be stored once in the system in logically shared memory. It does not need to be copied to each processor, which would otherwise waste time and/or space. Nor does the actual physical memory module location need to be specified by the programmer and sent to each processor. This is handled by the operating system (or hardware) as if the collection of memory modules is in one global address space (in the case of the Butterfly, for instance).

Secondly, the interconnection network performance in shared memory architectures is generally better suited for frequent communication of very small to very large packets of data. This is not usually the case for message passing machines. On the other hand, recent work described in [Nitz91] indicates that it is feasible to simulate a shared memory environment on a distributed memory parallel computer. In the future, this type of architecture/programming methodology might provide the type of scalable performance for which a graphics application would be well suited. Message passing architectures would be well suited to complex image generation algorithms such as ray tracing or radiosity because the cost of image generation is amortized when the task time is large in comparison to the data transfer time.

The performance of the Butterfly multistage interconnection network is much higher than the interconnection network in the iPSC, although the former is more costly. In addition, the Butterfly network can scale to large processor configurations, and therefore provide better performance than a bus-based shared memory system.

Since the Encore Multimax and other bus-based systems are limited in the number of processors they can support, low or normal quality image generation would fit well onto that type of architecture. Higher quality imagery demands more compute power as well as more memory than is normally available on bus architectures. One exception is the Alliant FX/28000, which uses up to 28 Intel i860 processors. The number of processors cannot be increased beyond this, but very high performance has been obtained on this system. Still, the Butterfly TC2000 is a faster version of the GP1000 and does provide the scalability necessary to render extremely large datasets. If judicious distribution of graphics data is used, memory latency can be reduced to a negligible overhead.

Although all of these architectures are suitable for graphics algorithms, the Butterfly environment provides a stronger case for high performance. In summary, with regard to the issues discussed previously, the BBN Butterfly is the best example of a shared memory multiprocessor which meets these requirements. The distributed memory modules within the Butterfly allow the programmer to take advantage of local memory access while a global view is provided of shared memory. The performance of the interconnection network and memory modules is better than a bus-based system such as the Encore Multimax, and the number of processors that the machine is capable of supporting allows massive parallelism.

The BBN Butterfly GP1000 at The Ohio State University's Computer and Information Science Department was used for the primary development and debugging of the algorithms presented in this book. This machine only had 10 processors, so it was desirable to test the programs on a larger machine. The Naval Research Lab, Georgia Institute of Technology, and Michigan State University all provided access to machines with larger configurations for this purpose. Final testing was done on the Butterfly GP1000 located at the headquarters of BBN Advanced Computers, Inc. This machine contains 107 processors, but we have limited testing of the programs to 96 processors. Under all circumstances, this machine was not being used by others at the time of testing, so no other processes interfered with the timings. The BBN TC2000 is their next generation multiprocessor which contains numerous enhancements to the design used in the GP1000. For some of the tests given in chapter 5, access was provided to a 47 processor TC2000 at Argonne National Laboratory, as well as to a 128 processor TC2000 at Lawrence Livermore National Laboratory. As a note to the reader, for further reference in the rest of this book, the term *processor* is used to denote a processor-memory module on the Butterfly.

3.3. The BBN Programming Environment

An algorithm can be designed to take advantage of a particular machine's characteristics to enhance overall performance. The algorithms illustrated here were designed for an MIMD architecture and optimized for implementation on the BBN Butterfly. Ideally, one would like to design program code so that it will run unmodified on a variety of parallel architectures. Although some parallel environments are available on a wide variety of machines (notably Linda [Ahuh86]), we did not have access to these programming tools. The parallel programming paradigms available on the Butterfly at Ohio State (where the code was originally developed) are BBN's Uniform System and a version of C-Threads originally developed at Carnegie-Mellon University [Coop87]. Additionally, Lawrence Livermore provides a split-join programming model called PCP, but it is currently only supported on the TC2000 [Gord91], and not the GP1000.

The Uniform System approach is a BBN specific parallel programming scheme [BBN89a]. This method uses the concept of generators which spawn off parallel tasks in a number of different ways selectable by the programmer. The second paradigm is C-Threads, which was ported to the Butterfly at The Ohio State University [Sami89]. The Uniform System was used for implementation purposes since it is supported by BBN and the program code would be able to run unmodified on the TC2000 as well.

The Uniform System parallel programming paradigm is designed to allow the programmer to develop parallel applications which are insensitive to the actual number of processors in the system. The program code does not need to be modified, nor special cases taken into account when it is run under different processor configurations. This also allows for debugging and testing on a small number of processors and later using all of the processors in the system for timing measurements. The Uniform System is a library of routines that the user links with in a C or Fortran program. In the case of the algorithms presented here, all of the code is written in C. The Uniform System can basically be divided into two sections: the shared memory portion and the task assignment portion. In addition, special routines are available to handle atomic operations, locks for synchronization, spin waits, and other configuration operators. Memory can be allocated in the system as:

1. Local variables
2. Global variables
3. Dynamic storage
4. Shared dynamic storage
5. Copied storage

Local, global, and dynamically allocated memory are treated the same as in any normal C program, with each processor having its own copy of a variable. Processor i and processor j may both reference a variable l, but its value is different on each processor since each has its own local copy.

Shared dynamic storage allows one to create space for data which can be stored somewhere in global memory. The data is available to each processor, but is only stored physically in one processor's memory module so that if processor i updates the value to shared variable s, processor j would also see the new value. Of course, synchronization must be used to correctly update a shared variable if two processors could possibly change it simultaneously. Routines exist in the Uniform System where a shared variable can be specified to be stored on a particular memory module (for instance the local processor's module) or scattered somewhere in the system. This allows the programmer to create efficient access to shared memory and to prevent hot spot contention. Hot spot contention occurs when a large number of remote references backup on a single switch node, causing delays in the network. The process node controller (PNC) on the processor board determines the location of a shared memory reference and handles the message traffic to complete the write or read operation. The memory allocator forces all shared memory to be allocated to locations which are above a given virtual address fence register.

The last type of storage, copied storage, allows data to be copied to all of the processors, effectively providing local access to a common variable. After the variable is copied, each processor has its own local copy of the variable so a modification will not be propagated to all the other processors, as in the shared memory case. This method is used to copy read-only data to all processors. It is also used to allow processors to know the location of a shared memory variable. As an example, a processor allocates a shared variable and places a value in the memory location, only that particular processor knows which memory location is used in shared storage. In order to allow the other processors to know the location, a call is made to the Uniform System routine *Share*, which propagates the *address* of the shared variable to all of the other processors so that they all can refer to the single memory location. The *Share* routine can also be used to just copy data, so instead of propagating the address of the variable, the value of the variable itself is propagated. The latter method of usage is an example of the copied storage approach.

Task assignment in the Uniform System is handled by a mechanism known as *task generators* which is a distributed task assignment system that works as follows. A program starts off running on a single processor. When a parallel environment is created on P processors, shared memory can be allocated and the other $(P - 1)$ processors start a spin-loop where they execute code that detects if there are any tasks available to work on. As soon as a generator (a procedure initializing a parallel environment) is executed by the first processor, a specified number of processors (any number from 1 to P with the choice of inclusion of the initiating processor) execute a task activator procedure to generate the next task. If a parallel *for* loop is desired, the task activator would consist of an atomic operation which increments the *for* loop index. As soon as the index is atomically updated on processor i, that processor begins work using the index as a parameter to a worker procedure. This happens throughout the system so that each processor essentially finds work for itself rather than using a central controlling mechanism. As soon as a worker is finished, that processor tries to find additional work by checking the task activator again. Note that more than one task activator can be running at the same time by using recursive generator calls, although the order of execution is difficult to predict. When all of the tasks are exhausted, the generator finishes, and if no other generators have created tasks, the initial processor proceeds serially while the others spin-wait until more work comes along.

3.4. Summary

In the first section of this chapter, a number of multiprocessor architectures are presented for the purpose of examining their characteristics with regard to a graphics display algorithm. In the second section, criteria for evaluation of these architectures is given, and each type of machine (of which all were available for testing) is scrutinized based on its characteristics and suitability for implementation of a parallel graphics algorithm. The BBN Butterfly is shown to be the computer most suitable for implementation of a parallel graphics display algorithm. In the third section, the Butterfly programming environment is described to give the reader a better understanding of its operational characteristics from a software point of view.

The next chapter describes the serial algorithm upon which the different parallel decompositions are based. In addition, timing measurements as well as measurements of performance analysis are discussed.

4

Overview of Base Level Implementation

In this chapter, we describe the choices that were made for a base level implementation of the different parallel graphics decompositions. The approach used for developing the parallel programs is to devise a single basis graphics rendering algorithm, and then build different parallel task partitioning and memory referencing schemes on top of it. This allows an equal comparison of a number of different approaches for parallelism since the underlying algorithm is the same. This basis algorithm is not compromised by the parallel algorithms since it can be modified to the specifics of each particular parallel approach. The first section of this chapter presents this basis algorithm by describing the underlying serial approach, as well as the choices that were made which were common to all of the parallel formulations. The second section of this chapter describes the measurement techniques used to obtain timings for the different programs. The last section gives the performance analysis measures used to analyze the different parallel implementations that are presented in the next chapter.

4.1. Design of the Basis Algorithm

The purpose of implementing a number of parallel graphics rendering algorithms is to analyze different parallel work decompositions and shared memory referencing schemes to determine which method is the most viable for general use. In order to make a straightforward comparison of the possible decompositions, a serial algorithm has been developed upon which the various parallel formulations are based. Most parallel rendering algorithms developed in the past were designed similarly. Essentially, some portion of the parallel algorithm consists of a single task resembling a serial algorithm in a smaller context. This approach makes it easier to compare the parallel implementations because their relative speed for the basic portion of the algorithm is the same. This may seem like we are compromising the aspects of a parallel machine by using smaller serial tasks, but such is not the case. It just turns out that for this type of problem, the solutions presented are the most straightforward and yield the highest performance compared with a functional work decomposition.

Based on the taxonomy and algorithm analysis presented in chapter 2, several variations on an image space parallel decomposition have been implemented. Each single task of the parallel algorithms consists of solving the rendering problem in a serial manner for a particular area of the image space. Chapter 5 describes these algorithms, which vary in their method of task assignment to processors, area size, and memory referencing characteristics. In this chapter, the basis sequential algorithm for the front end and the single task tiling portion are described.

This serial basis algorithm is a scan line Z-buffer algorithm [Myer75] which incorporates the stochastic sampling method [Cook86] for anti-aliasing as an extension. The serial algorithm used here was originally developed separately as part of a project to enable scientists to render polygonal datasets at varying degrees of accuracy. Several different anti-aliasing methods can be used including a straight Z-buffer, an analytic method, and a stochastic sampling method with 16 samples per pixel. In addition, several illumination models are available, including those developed by Gouraud [Gour71], Phong [Phon75], Blinn [Blin77], and Cook-Torrance [Cook82]. The rendering method which is used for the comparison tests incorporates stochastic sampling for anti-aliasing with the Blinn shading model using various images rendered at a resolution of 640 x 484. We will elaborate on the test scenes in section 4.2.1.

As stated previously, each algorithm involves a break-up of the image space into different areas, and the image rendering problem is essentially solved serially in a given area. Clipping is done initially for the entire screen, but for each individual area, single scan line clipping is used instead of polygon clipping to the area boundaries. It might be interesting to compare scan line versus polygon clipping, but this would only minimally affect the overall performance of the algorithms.

4.1.1. Front End

The files which are used for the test object data are called *detail* files. This format was developed at The Ohio State University Computer Graphics Research Group (now known as the Advanced Computing Center for Arts and Design) in the 1970s. This format is fairly compact and the data in the file is stored in binary. The format is shown here:

```
num_pts num_polys
x1 y1 z1
x2 y2 z2
 .
 .
 .
num_vertices point1 point2 point3 ...
num_vertices point1 point2 point3 ...
 .
 .
 .
```

The number of points and number of polygons are 16 bit integers, which means that only 32,767 points and polygons are allowed in a single object. The points list follows these two values, and each point is represented as three floating point values. After that, the polygon list includes the number of vertices in a polygon and indices to the points list above. An edge is implied between adjacent vertices in the list. The polygons are guaranteed to be convex, and it is assumed that the last vertex listed for a polygon is connected to the first by an edge. Since the object detail files limit the number of vertices and polygons, larger objects must be broken up into smaller objects so that the same format may be used.

The front end of each parallel graphics program consists of the following phases:

1. Read in object data files from disk.
2. Perform necessary transformations.
3. Reject back-facing polygons and clip polygons to screen borders.
4. Place polygons into shared data structure.

A parallel pipelined implementation of this front end is described in the following subsections.

4.1.1.1. Reading in Objects

It was necessary to modify the detail file format so that the regular objects could be broken up into sub-objects to allow sufficient parallelism in the front end. This allows the object data to be distributed across the memories of the processors. In order to do this, a separate program was written which reads in an object file and creates a new object file, consisting of the same original object but subdivided into components. The sub-object size is determined based on the number of polygons in the original object; it can be as small as 100 polygons for simple objects and increases to 1000 polygons for more complex objects. The only problem with subdividing the object is that the original normals at the vertices need to be kept with the points since a new normal calculated for a sub-object alone could be incorrect.

An incorrect normal would be calculated in the following scenario. A polygon which was previously part of the original object is moved into a new sub-object. The normal of this polygon will no longer influence the vertex normals of its neighbors unless this normal is calculated prior to the subdivision of the object and copied along with its vertex. Thus, the untransformed vertex normals are calculated and stored with the sub-object directly after the points list in each file. This creates a somewhat larger data file format, but is the only solution that allows distributing the objects across memories. There is a slight problem with storing the untransformed normal if the object transformation from object space to eye space includes non-uniform scaling operations, so this situation was prevented from occurring in the test cases used here. The time for manipulating the datafiles prior to program execution is not accounted for in the timings since this is just a variation of the original object format which could be output from any data generation package.

4.1.1.2. Parallelizing the Front End

The diagram in figure 4.1 illustrates how phases 1, 2, and 3 of the front end can be overlapped in parallel execution. When a processor is available to do a read operation, it performs a single pass check of a global array to see how much data is currently stored on all the other processors. If a given processor contains fewer polygons than the average of all the processors, then this processor puts itself on the queue to read an object from disk into its own local memory.

The number of polygons read in and determined to be front facing is then stored in a global array. By using this scheme, the input data is scattered among all the memory modules in roughly equal portions. The data is also sharable so that all processors have access to it. After the data is read in on a given processor, the disk is available for the next processor to access. This algorithm creates a pipeline which is faster than serially processing the data and distributing it.

This scattering of polygons allows a nearly uniform scattering of data as well as work for the front end, so that each processor's work is approximately of time complexity $O(N/P)$ where N is the total number of polygons read in. For datasets which are small, the pipeline does not become completely saturated if the number of sub-objects is less than the number of processors. This situation would not provide enough work for all of the processors during the front end phases, nor would the object data get completely scattered throughout the

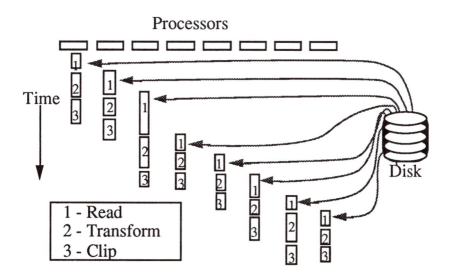

Figure 4.1: Overlapped disk access with front end phases

memories in the system. For the test cases here, we were not interested in completely optimizing the front end; it was developed merely as an efficient method to read-in and scatter the object datasets. Obviously this portion of the program needs to be optimized for each combination of object data format and chosen hardware. The method given here is a general outline of one way to parallelize this section of code.

The front end should be optimized depending on the intended application of the renderer. For animated sequences, reading in data is only necessary when a new object enters the scene for a given frame. More optimization might be spent on the transformation and clipping phases for this application. If still images are required, it might be desirable to optimize the entire front end. Regardless, it can be seen that it is worthwhile to parallelize this section of the parallel program.

This example parallelization of the front end is the same for all of the algorithms described herein. The only difference occurs in the section where polygons are put into data structures depending on their screen space location, as described in section 4.1.1.3. Since this latter portion of the front end of each parallel algorithm may be slightly different in complexity, we include the time differences for this portion of the front end in our overall algorithm analysis in chapter 6. The data structure used for storing the polygons according to their location is described in the next subsection.

4.1.1.3. Placing Polygons in Shared Data Structure

Each of the parallel algorithms is a variation on an area screen space subdivision algorithm. Prior to the parallel tiling and rendering phases, the polygons must be tagged as to which subdivision(s) they belong to. The polygons are placed in a data structure which is shared among all of the processors so that each processor can obtain the exact polygons relevant to any subdivision. Each parallel decomposition scheme employs an approach in placing the data in this structure that is slightly different than the one used in a traditional serial scan line algorithm. In a serial approach, this section consists of loading polygons into an array of linked lists called a y-bucket list (see [Roge85] for details on how this is done). Each linked list (or y-bucket) corresponds to a scan line and contains pointers to polygons which have their minimum y-extent on that particular scan line. During the tiling section of a serial algorithm, the program investigates the active y-bucket to determine which new polygons start on the given scan line and should be stored in the active polygon list. For the parallel image space decompositions, it is necessary to do a pre-culling operation prior to creating a y-bucket list for a given area on the screen. This pre-culling operation involves loading the polygons into an *area bucket* data structure so that it is possible to find out which polygons are relevant to a given area on the screen, not just a single scan line.

Although the various parallel algorithms rely on different size areas for their partitions, the basic culling operation is similar in each. The area bucket list is used to store polygons for the areas which will later become separate parallel tasks in the tiling section. During the front end, the bounding box of each polygon read in by a processor is checked against the area mesh created for the given parallel decomposition. A pointer to the polygon is then stored in each area bucket that the bounding box crosses. The polygons are not clipped to these areas, nor is a more stringent test employed to see if the actual polygon (not just its bounding box) intersects the area. Although a stricter test could be used, the approach used here is fast and uncomplicated, with the only drawback being lack of accuracy. In other words, a polygon's bounding box might cross over an area in which the polygon itself is not actually present. The common thread to this portion of the program, which is the same for all the parallel formulations, is that the area bucket list is a shared data structure available to all processors. As the polygons are read in during the front end, each processor determines the appropriate area bucket to place a shared pointer to the polygon. A lock is used to prevent more than one processor from placing the pointer into the same area bucket list at the same time. This constitutes what we will call the Uniformly Distributed (UD) memory referencing scheme since the polygons themselves are scattered throughout global memory, in addition to a scattering of the polygon pointers in the area bucket data structure.

As was mentioned previously, each partitioning scheme implements this section of the front end in a slightly different manner since the size and number of areas is dependent on the parallel partitioning scheme. Specific details on the usage of the area bucket data structure are given with each individual algorithm description in chapter 5.

4.1.2. Tiling

The tiling section of a scan line based graphics rendering algorithm is the most time consuming portion of this type of program. It consists primarily of the following phases:

For each scan line in an area:
1. Determine which polygons are new to the current scan line.
2. Build edge lists for those polygons and determine which edge pairs start on the current scan line.
3. Update any edge pairs from the previous scan line in which one or both of the original edges in the pair is no longer active.
4. Interpolate vertically from the previous scan line to the current scan line for all parameters, such as edge position, color, and normal.
5. Perform hidden surface elimination and anti-aliasing.
6. Shade the fragments which are visible within each pixel for the scan line.
7. Send finished scan line out to the frame buffer.
8. Deactivate polygons, edge pairs, and edge lists which end on the current scan line.

In a traditional serial approach, the area refers to the entire screen and each scan line is the width of the screen. In the case of a parallel image space algorithm, an area is a single task and a scan line is the width of that area (each area may be different in size, though). We will now systematically go through each of the preceding phases, pointing out the choices made which are common to all of the parallel implementations.

In the tiling phase, a task corresponding to a particular area on the screen is obtained by a processor. The polygons which are relevant to this area are stored in an area bucket in shared memory during the front end. During the tiling phase, this processor determines which polygons to work with by examining the appropriate area bucket. The polygons which are in this area bucket are loaded into that processor's local memory y-bucket list. The y-bucket list contains the pointers to the polygons in shared memory. Since some polygons could have started above the first scan line of the area, these polygons are stored in the top scan line y-bucket for that area. Phase 1 of the tiling operation involves traversing the y-bucket for the current scan line and extracting those polygons which start on this scan line.

Phase 2 involves building the edge lists and edge pairs and storing them in the processor's local memory. These are put in local memory because this type of access is much faster than remotely referencing the data. There are several reasons why this is wasteful, however. If a polygon crosses the boundaries of more than one area, the edge lists are constructed for each area in addition to the duplication of memory required to store these data structures in each processor's local memory. It is possible to store these data structures in shared memory but the following complications could arise. Synchronization would be required if two processors try to build the same edge lists at the same time. In addition, although the initial interpolation parameters and delta values are the same for a duplicated edge, the current value of an interpolation parameter depends on which scan line is active for each processor sharing the edge. It is likely that the active scan line is different in each processor. Consequently, the memory savings of storing the data in each processor's local memory is more than offset by the additional remote referencing cost that would otherwise be incurred. Therefore, although the local referencing method may be slightly wasteful in memory usage and involve duplication to build some data structures, it is superior in speed. As a result, the tiling portion of the program will execute faster and the interconnection network will not be used.

Phase 3 (updating the edge pairs) of the tiling operation proceeds as in a traditional scan line algorithm, and no remote referencing is incurred here. Phase 4 (scan line interpolation) is also the same as a serial method with no remote referencing. Phase 5 (hidden surface removal) involves the use of a stochastic sampling anti-aliasing technique which allows hidden surface removal and anti-aliasing to occur simultaneously. Some remote referencing is required in the Uniformly Distributed memory referencing scheme to obtain the plane equation for a given polygon from shared memory. Phase 6 (shading) involves performing the illumination calculation on the visible polygon fragments left over from phase 5. After the fragments' colors are determined, a box filter is used to convolve the fragments with each pixel to determine the overall pixel color. At the current time, the filter is limited to the width of a single pixel since it is difficult to handle pixels which are beyond the border of the current area in a parallel environment. An area for future work might include applying a Gaussian filter which extends beyond a single pixel boundary. After the the pixel colors are determined, they are loaded into a single scan line buffer and block transferred to the virtual frame buffer in phase 7. The block transfer is faster than updating each pixel in the virtual frame buffer one at a time. After this phase, the polygons, edges, and edge pairs which expire on the current scan line are deactivated in phase 8. More information on how the scan line data is stored in the frame buffer and how it is written out is included in the next subsection.

4.1.3. Back End

Since the areas on the screen are computed in a random order which depends on the scheduling of tasks onto processors, full scan lines cannot be output onto the frame buffer during the computation of the image. On the other hand, each individual area could be output as it is calculated, but this is distracting to the user, in addition to creating additional network traffic. The solution then, is to store the frame buffer internally in memory and output the pixel data after the tiling is completed. This is accomplished in the following manner. A virtual frame buffer is stored in the physical memory of the machine by scattering the rows of the frame buffer among the different memory modules. This allows uniform scattering of the data and avoids hot spot contention. As stated previously, rather than have the processors directly write pixel values to remote memory, each processor contains a small local memory buffer corresponding to the width of a scan line. After an area-width scan line is finished, this buffer is block transferred from local memory to its place in the globally shared virtual frame buffer. This continues throughout the tiling portion of the program. At the end of the tiling operation, the virtual frame buffer is completely filled and can be displayed.

After the image has been calculated, each scan line is compressed using run-length encoding. Run-length encoding allows the image to be stored using less space than is required with a simple pixel map method. This operation is done in parallel but no information is kept from one scan line to the next, though this would be done in a sequential implementation. As the run-length encoding is proceeding, each processor checks a shared variable that indicates the current scan line which is available to write out to disk. If the variable indicates that a given processor's scan line can be written out, that processor writes out the run-length encoded scan line and proceeds to find more scan lines to process. This allows the image to be written out in scan line order while the run-length encoding is performed in parallel. Of course, the scan line order forces a bottleneck situation, but this is the only way the image can be written out. Modifications to this section of the program would allow tuning to a particular application.

The preceding descriptions above constitute the basis serial algorithm and parallel extensions which are common to all of the parallel partitioning schemes. These schemes are outlined in detail in chapter 5 and compared to each other, along with an evaluation of shared memory referencing in chapter 6. The next section is a description of the testing procedures and performance analysis methods employed in the analysis of the algorithms.

4.2. Testing Procedures

In this section, we discuss how the algorithms are evaluated according to a number of criteria. The scenes which are used to test the various algorithms are described, as is the timing procedure utilized.

4.2.1. Test Scenes

It is important that the three-dimensional scenes which are used as test data accurately reflect what might occur in everyday usage of a graphics display program. Since it is hard to imagine what an "average" scene might entail, numerous researchers have developed their own methods of analyzing algorithms by providing a number of test circumstances. The only unfortunate aspect of this situation is that the data is not available to other researchers to test their own programs on. To rectify this situation, Eric Haines has developed what he calls the standard procedural database (SPD), which is used for the sole purpose of testing rendering algorithms [Hain87a]. His intended application was ray tracing, but these scenes can be used for testing any display algorithm. Among the scenes available are: a group of balls, a set of gears, a tetrahedron, a tree, a group of rings, and a fractal mountain. Each scene can be generated to create as many polygons as the user desires since the programs create the database procedurally. It was decided to test the algorithms here using small to large databases. The tree was generated with approximately 106,000 polygons, while the mountain was generated with 131,000 polygons. Haines has given view parameters as well which are also part of the database specification. In the case of the mountain image, a much denser version was created than Haines used in his testing (his mountain only contained 8K polygons). Using his viewing matrix, a majority of the polygons would have been clipped out of the scene. To rectify this, a new view matrix was constructed to allow the entire mountain to be seen. The 4 x 4 matrix used for viewing is included in the appendix in equation A.1.

It was also desirable to test the algorithms on some real world type data, so we used a stegosaurus image which was designed for an animation and a Chrysler Laser automobile which was designed from a CAD/CAM program. The stegosaurus is not rendered with its plates since they were unavailable at the time of testing. The stegosaurus contains approximately 10,000 polygons, while the automobile contains approximately 46,000 polygons. The stegosaurus data was created by John Donkin of ACCAD (the Ohio State University Advanced Computing Center for the Arts and Design) for the Fernbank Museum in Atlanta. The car was created by Chrysler and obtained from Evans & Sutherland Computer Corporation. All tests were performed at a resolution of 640 x 484 using Blinn's [Blin77] light model for the specular component. An illustration of these images appears in color plate 1.

In chapter 6, higher density images were used to test the algorithms with more demanding data. For these tests, a version of Haines' rings database was created with approximately 568,000 polygons, and a denser version of the tree database was generated with 851,000 polygons.

4.2.2. Timing

It is important to state how the programs were timed on the system to show what is included in the performance graphs given later in this book. On a multiprocessor such as the Intel iPSC, program code must be loaded into all of the processors prior to running the program itself. On the Butterfly, this is not the case. The Butterfly is a virtual memory machine, and the program code is paged into memory as it is needed [BBN89a]. Prior to starting a parallel environment, the first processor contains the resident code and any allocated memory. When a parallel environment is started and a processor references a page of memory or program code that is not resident in that processor's local memory module, this item is paged in automatically. The first time this happens, it may occur almost simultaneously on all processors since they will likely be executing the same code at the start of a parallel environment. A bottleneck situation occurs since all of the processors are trying to obtain pages of program code at nearly the same time. Although this method is significantly faster than the loading operation in the iPSC (primarily due to the speed and topology of the Butterfly interconnect), any timings which include this startup cost are somewhat misleading since they do not indicate the true performance of the machine. An adequate solution used by most researchers is to run the parallel portion a second time within the program itself and evaluate program performance for this second iteration only. This method is used for the results given in chapter 5.

Another overhead is encountered due to the implementation of the Uniform System on the Butterfly which occurs when a task generator is called for the first time. This is due to the fact that all of the processors need to be notified that a generator is available for execution, and this takes $O(P)$ time. To alleviate this effect, each processor starts off its first task inside the generator by hitting a barrier. Once all processors have hit the barrier, the processors are released and the timing starts. On the Butterfly GP1000, a time of approximately 2 seconds has been measured for our maximum test configuration of 96 processors to hit this barrier. This time is seen only once at the onset of a generator and would not be present in other parallel programming models.

The timing mechanism used on the GP1000 is a routine called *getrtc* (get real-time clock) which gives time increments of 64.5 μsec. On the TC2000, the clock ticks are accurate to 1 μsec. The performance of all algorithms is evaluated using these routines from within the program. There is no differentiation between system time and program time since during most of these tests, no other processes were running besides the normal MACH system processes. The Uniform System ensures that only one user process is assigned to a processor, resulting in no interference caused by other user processes. The nature of interprocessor communication and overhead due to system processes can change the performance, and as a result, the same test run multiple times can vary by several tenths of a second. In most cases, this amounts to less than 1% of the total parallel time, so we did not rerun the programs to obtain an average time. This was done in all cases except in the case of the final timing on 96 processors which was averaged over five runs for additional accuracy. The tests consumed much CPU time and took many months of programmer time to initiate and gather results.

4.3. Performance Analysis

Various graphics researchers in the past have written simulators in software to verify their parallel algorithms which may have been designed for hardware or a conventional multiprocessor. At the time of their research, the hardware was either not available or was too costly to obtain for actual tests. Unfortunately, some very real factors such as communication, network contention, and load balancing cannot be fully analyzed in a simulated environment.

The first subsection here describes the measures usually used to gauge performance of a parallel program: time, speedup, and efficiency. The value of these factors is that they provide an indication of the actual realized performance, relative parallel performance, and processor utilization, respectively. It is not sufficient to look at any one of these measurements alone since one might be misled by not observing the whole picture.

In the context of parallelizing a circuit simulation application, Sadayappan and Visvanathan [Sada88] develop a framework where the overall performance of a parallel algorithm is evaluated by breaking it down into relevant component factors. It would be desirable to develop a similar framework to interpret performance of a parallel graphics algorithm in terms of quantitative measures characterizing relevant factors.

A number of overhead factors are introduced when a program is implemented on a parallel architecture and these are outlined in the second subsection. In some cases, these factors relate to the machine itself, and in other cases they relate to the changes necessary to allow the program to run in parallel. Initially, a program is modified or specifically designed for implementation on a parallel architecture. The changes represent the differences between the serial and parallel versions of the program. While these changes are introduced by the programmer, additional overhead factors are introduced by the fact that a particular machine architecture is used and communication is necessary to allow the processors to work on the problem simultaneously.

4.3.1. Time, Speedup, and Efficiency

Due to the size of the datasets, the 4 megabyte limit in memory per processor (on the GP1000), and the size of the data structures needed for algorithm storage, it was necessary to initiate the timing tests above one processor. The reason this was done was to avoid paging during the computation if the datasets did not fit into physical memory. Since there is only a single disk on the Butterfly, paging would cause a serial bottleneck which would not provide realistic parallel timings for the given datasets. By checking to see if a given timing run is paging (using the MACH command vmstat), the minimum number of processors which can be used without paging effects can be determined. This minimum number for each dataset is as follows: 2 processors for the stegosaurus image, 6 processors for the Laser image, and 12 processors for the tree and mountain images. These minimum processor configurations are used since it is not possible to determine the amount of time incurred due to paging and then eliminate that time from the results.

The potential speedup in a parallel algorithm is calculated by the formula given in equation 4.1 (also called *Amdahl's law* [Amda67]).

$$\frac{T(1)}{T(P)} = \frac{(s+p)}{\left(s+\dfrac{p}{P}\right)}$$

$$(4.1)$$

$T(x)$ is the computation time on x processors, P is the number of processors, s is the sequential portion of the computation, and p is the parallel portion (identified on one processor). If $s = 0$, then we have obtained linear speedup. The potential speedup as given in Amdahl's law is limited by the sequential portion of the program. If one assumes that s and p are percentage values, then we can rewrite the law with a numerator of 1 since the total computation time on 1 processor adds up to 100%.

Amdahl's law has gained acceptance as a predictor of the maximum expected speedup of parallel algorithms on multiprocessors. In a sense, this law expresses doubt about the amount of speedup attainable by parallel algorithms on real machines. The doubt is well-founded since most algorithms involve some inherently sequential portions of code. Operations such as synchronization of processes, message passing delays, and memory latency also reduce the potential parallelism.

For parallel programs, Amdahl's law can be applied if we know the serial percentage of the algorithm for a given value of P. Often, this is difficult to calculate prior to running the program on P processors, but it does serve as a good indicator of performance if we calculate the percentages after running the program. Instead, the speedup is used as a guideline to relative program performance as the number of processors is increased. Equation 4.2 shows how speedup is normally determined. The time using 1 processor for a parallel program and its single memory module is divided by the time using P processors and P memory modules. This is indicated in equation 4.2 where $T_x(y)$ refers to the time using x memory modules on y processors. The speedup is basically an indication of the effective number of processors utilized.

$$\text{Speedup} = \frac{T_1(1)}{T_P(P)}$$

$$(4.2)$$

The minimum number of processors (MIN) in which each test scene fits into the physical memory of the machine without paging precludes direct testing of the algorithms on one processor to determine speedup (recall MIN is image dependent). Instead, a work-around solution is used to evaluate the time that the algorithms would take if they could be run on a single processor with enough physical memory.

The programs are started for each image on MIN number of processors so that there is enough physical memory available without paging. The data is read in, transformed, and clipped using this number of processors, which incorporates the Uniformly Distributed memory scattering scheme. The tiling section is run using only one processor, however. This processor retrieves the data from global memory as is necessary. This would be the fastest method to run each sequential algorithm on the physical machine, given the amount of memory actually available per processor. Equation 4.3 is used to calculate the estimated speedup on 96 processors.

$$\text{Estimated Speedup} = \frac{T_{\text{MIN}}(1)}{T_{96}(96)}$$

(4.3)

Efficiency is calculated using equation 4.4, where P_{max} is the maximum number of processors used for testing (here, P_{max} = 96). Efficiency is an indication of the utilization of the processors in the system.

$$\text{Efficiency} = \frac{\text{Estimated Speedup}}{P_{max}}$$

(4.4)

For the results shown in chapter 5, the time and speedup graphs are shown only for the tiling section of the programs since this is the most time consuming, as well as the most parallelizable portion of the program. In chapter 6, a comparison of all the algorithms' times is included, along with the time for the initial startup operations from the front end which are specific to each approach. This gives us a fair basis for comparison of each of the algorithms. The total front end and back end times are not included, although considerable effort was spent in parallelizing this portion of the code. The reason is that the optimization of this portion of the code would be handled differently depending on the application intended.

Next we describe a number of different overhead factors and their effects on a parallel program.

4.3.2. Overhead of Parallel versus Serial Implementation

Factors which are introduced by the difference between the uniprocessor and multiprocessor version of the programs include: scheduling, memory latency, communication utilizing block transfers, over-head due to adaptation of the algorithm for parallel execution, load imbalance, contention, and synchronization. In this section, we describe each overhead factor and the testing method used to evaluate each factor's impact on the algorithms presented in chapter 5. The testing method used to determine each overhead factor is generally common to all of the parallel algorithms presented in chapter 5, but some differences in measurement occur due to the nature of these algorithms. These differences are elaborated upon at their point of reference in chapter 5. All of the testing to evaluate these overheads was done at 96 processors since the maximum number of processors used provides the worst case scenario as far as the overhead factors are concerned. It should also be noted that this testing was done separate from the performance timing for the algorithms.

The different overhead factors discussed in this subsection are determined as a percentage of the total processor-time space, as shown in figure 4.2.

Each processor may take a different amount of time to complete its work. The leftover time is idle time, as is illustrated in the figure. The time when the last of P processors finishes its work is $T(P)$ or just Tp. There may be a number of different ways of evaluating the overhead factors, but the method chosen here is to determine a percentage value of the overhead with respect to the total processor-time space $(P * Tp)$. This expression is used as the denominator in the

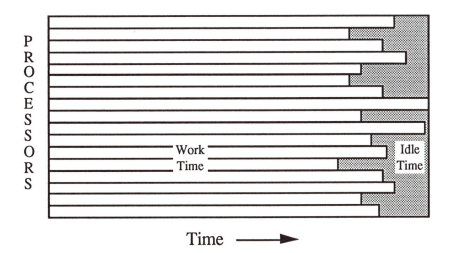

Figure 4.2: Processor-time space

equations since a processor must wait until all other processors are finished before it is able to work on some other job outside of the given program. The overhead percentage value should be taken to mean the effect of the overhead on the total processor-time space.

4.3.2.1. Scheduling

In discussing scheduling overhead, we first describe our definition of this effect and then go over the mechanism by which tasks are assigned in the Uniform System. Scheduling overhead in a parallel context refers to the time it takes for a given task to be scheduled by the system. In this case, it is assumed that a parallel environment has already been started and a set of tasks are available for execution. Scheduling is accomplished by use of a critical section which must be executed by one processor at a time. The time of scheduling overhead for a single task is the amount of time it takes to run through this critical section.

Scheduling in the Uniform System works by dynamic task assignment, as stated previously. A worker routine constitutes an individual task that is called with a given parameter list. The example used previously referred to a parallel version of a *for* loop as shown below:

```
for (i = 0; i < range; i++)
        do_work(i);
```

The Uniform System code to accomplish this involves calling the generator as shown below:

```
GenOnI(do_work, range);
```

One processor calls the generator GenOnI, and then all processors request work from this generator. The non-deterministic nature of dynamic scheduling insures that processors are assigned individual iterations of the *for* loop and execute the routine do_work for their given iteration. The Uniform System provides other generators which can generate tasks in a more complex manner; this example just illustrates how a simple one works.

The Uniform System generator mechanism is fairly efficient and easy to use, but there do exist some overheads. The real overhead in scheduling that occurs in parallel programs is the entering of the critical section for obtaining the next task. In this case, scheduling tasks consists of incrementing the shared loop index and assigning the next task to an available processor. Using the Uniform System,

Plate 1. Test images for parallel programs: tree, stegosaurus, Laser, and mountain.

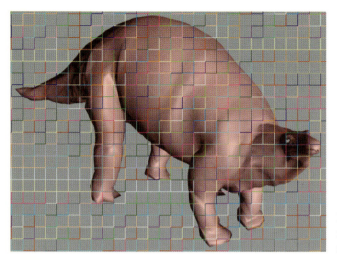

Plate 2a. Rectangular, data non-adaptive decomposition scheme.

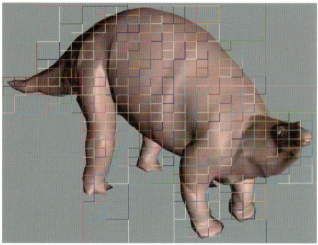

Plate 2b. Top-down, data adaptive decomposition scheme.

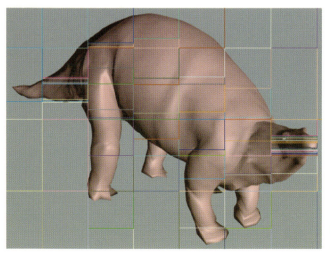

Plate 2c. Task adaptive decomposition scheme.

Plate 3.   Rings image.

Plate 4.   Dense tree image.

the time has been measured as 24 µsec on the GP1000 for a single task (call this T_{crit}). The scheduling is an inherent sequential process, so a task must take longer than $P * T_{crit}$ for a bottleneck due to scheduling to be avoided. On 96 processors, the minimum task time which would limit bottlenecks due to scheduling needs to be at least 2.3 msec (denoted T_{sched}). The scheduling overhead for the various images is the total time devoted to scheduling tasks divided by the total parallel execution time, as shown in equation 4.5.

$$\text{Scheduling \%} = \frac{\sum_{i=0}^{P-1} i \cdot T_{crit} + (N - P) \cdot T_{crit}}{T_p \cdot P} * 100 \%$$

(4.5)

For the ith processor to start working, it has to wait for $(i - 1)$ tasks to be scheduled before it. It therefore takes a total time of $(i \cdot T_{crit})$ to be scheduled. Summing this up for all processors yields the first term in the numerator in equation 4.5. The second term is the additional scheduling time required for each of the $(N - P)$ tasks left after the first one is scheduled for each processor (N is the total number of tasks to be scheduled) assuming that each task takes more than $(P - 1) \cdot T_{crit}$ time to execute. Thus, a key factor in evaluating scheduling overhead involves making sure that no bottleneck results from a task taking less than $(P - 1) \cdot T_{crit}$ to execute. For a graphics algorithm, the minimum task time is based on sending the background color to the virtual frame buffer. Therefore, this time is measured to see if there is potentially a bottleneck. The denominator is the total processor-time space where T_p is the ending parallel execution time on the maximum processor configuration.

4.3.2.2. Memory Latency

Memory latency in a multiprocessor refers to the extra time required to send (write) or send and receive (read) a request for/from remote memory. This time is somewhat dependent on the number of switch nodes the message must travel through, but since we are dealing with a 4 column switch on the test GP1000, the times measured are as follows: a 4 byte read takes 7 µsec, while a 4 byte write takes 4 µsec. In contrast, a local read takes 0.53 µsec, while a local write takes 0.38 µsec.

Memory latency can be measured by counting the number of remote references during program execution and adding up the additional time of remote versus local referencing time required for all of those references. This is done by using one of the Uniform System library calls which can detect if a given shared memory reference is a reference to a local or a remote memory module. The memory latency overhead (latency %) is determined by using equation 4.6.

$$\text{Latency \%} = \frac{\left[\# \text{ refs } * (T_{rref}(P) - T_{lref}(P))\right]}{T_p \bullet P} * 100 \%$$

(4.6)

In the equation, #refs is the average number of remote references per task, T_{rref} refers to the remote reference time, T_{lref} refers to the local reference time, and, as before, T_p is the ending time in parallel on the maximum processor configuration.

4.3.2.3. Communication

Although any kind of message traffic across the network could be termed *communication*, with regard to the BBN Butterfly, we are specifically referring to messages which are initiated using the machine's block transfer mechanism. This mechanism is built into the hardware of the GP1000 switch and allows a message path to stay open as long as necessary in order to get the message through. This requires a one time setup cost for the message of 8 μsec (T_{setup}) plus a cost of 0.25 μsec per byte transferred (T_{bt}) [BBN89b]. To alleviate blocking in the switch, block transfers are limited to 256 bytes and a software mechanism is provided to allow the programmer to use block transfers of longer messages. Since this cost is incurred once for a block of data and thereafter the data element is referenced locally, it is prudent to use block transfers if data can be partitioned into contiguous chunks. The cost of transferring these messages is the communication overhead but after this is taken into account, memory latency is no longer a factor since the data is available locally.

This overhead factor is derived by measuring the total number of bytes transferred in the system. Using the data for block transfer time for this number of bytes, taking into account that each message is a maximum of 256 bytes long, the total communication time is derived and shown in the numerator of equation 4.7.

$$\text{Comm. Overhead \%} = \frac{(\frac{\# \text{ bytes}}{256} \bullet T_{setup}) + (\# \text{ bytes} \bullet T_{bt})}{T_p \bullet P} * 100 \%$$

(4.7)

4.3.2.4. Overhead due to Adaptation for Parallelism

It is generally necessary to either modify a serial algorithm with parallel constructs or develop an entirely new parallel approach to run a program on a multiprocessor. There is an inherent overhead built into this new parallel algorithm which is not present in the serial algorithm. New constructs and task setup instructions used to achieve parallelism are required for the parallel implementation. For numerical parallel algorithms, this overhead is typically very small. For a graphics display algorithm, one of the benefits of executing in a sequential fashion is compromised: graphical coherence. When a large number of tasks is required, such as on 96 processors, the loss due to coherence may become a significant factor. The overhead due to adaptation for parallelism is measured as part of the total processor-time space as well; it primarily consists of loss due to the lack of coherence. The other portion of this overhead involves the additional setup costs for each task prior to its execution on a processor.

The overhead due to lack of coherence is directly related to the number of tasks in most cases. That is, if more tasks are used, more coherence is lost. Since this overhead is measured at the maximum processor configuration (which represents the most tasks for a particular algorithm), the loss due to coherence is highest and this represents the worst case scenario.

Different algorithms may have different amounts of this overhead. This fact should be taken into account when looking at the speedup graphs of a parallel algorithm. If the speedup curve is nearly linear but the overhead due to adaptation is large, the performance of a given algorithm may not be good in comparison to other algorithms if the other parallel algorithms have smaller overheads. If the speedup in an algorithm with a small loss due to coherence is better than another algorithms' speedup, it will eventually provide better parallel performance as P increases.

The overhead due to adaptation, or more accurately, the code modification overhead, can be measured in the following manner. A sequential algorithm with no code modification overhead is analogous to the situation of $T_{MIN}(1)$. Recall that $T_x(y)$ refers to a situation where x is the number of memory modules and y is the number of processors. If more than one area is used, the number of areas is subscripted afterward so that $T_x(y)_r$ refers to using r areas with x memory modules on y processors. The actual amount of work on P processors is thus $T_P(P)_{R \cdot P}$, where R is the granularity ratio ($R = \#tasks/P$). To simulate this work without any contention effects,

$T_{MIN}(1)_{R \cdot P}$ is measured since this gives the time overhead and if the communication cost is deducted, the actual computation cost is derived. The same is done for an essentially sequential task, which corresponds to $T_{MIN}(1)_1$. Subtracting the difference between these two values results in the exact extra work which is involved in setting up the tasks necessary for parallel execution. For instance, the coherence lost in both the vertical and horizontal directions is inherently included in this value. Equation 4.8 is used to measure this overhead based on the work assigned to P processors.

$$\text{Code Mod. Overhead } \% = \frac{T_{MIN}(1)_{R \cdot P} - T_{MIN}(1)_1}{T_p \cdot P} * 100 \%$$

(4.8)

4.3.2.5. Synchronization

Arvind and Ianucci [Arvi86] identify several basic synchronization situations:

a) *Producer-Consumer* - a data structure is produced by a given task to be used by another task on another processor. In order to insure that the consumer waits for the producer, synchronization must occur.

b) *Fork and Join* - a *join* operation indicates that two or more tasks have completed from a previous fork. To implement the join, a synchronization event must occur. The fork operation is basically a scheduling overhead, as discussed previously.

c) *Mutual Exclusion* - when two or more parallel tasks wish to execute a given region that only one is allowed in, this presents a critical section of the code which requires synchronization.

In the algorithms presented here, these situations do not come up that frequently in the tiling portion of the programs. The producer-consumer situation does occur in one algorithm but for the most part, the data structures used by the algorithms are mutually readable and very few are read-write. The overhead due to synchronization is measured as follows. The time in which a processor waits at a semaphore lock is summed up throughout the system. This time is indicated in the numerator in equation 4.9. The denominator is the total processor-time space as before.

$$\text{Synchronization } \% = \frac{\displaystyle\sum_{i=1}^{\#\,tasks} T^i_{synch}}{T_p \bullet P} * 100 \%$$

(4.9)

In the equation, T^i_{synch} refers to the synchronization wait time for task i. The fork operation occurs at the beginning of a generator, while the join operation occurs at the end of a generator. These factors are measured as part of the scheduling overhead and thus will not be a part of the synchronization measurement. Mutual exclusion is used for serial sections in the programs, but the measurements given here ignore the small serial sections at the beginning of the program.

4.3.2.6. Network Contention

Network contention refers to the slowdown incurred when more than one message attempts to use the same switch node at the same time. This can be categorized as the probability that a memory request will block at a switch node due to another message already using the given path. BBN refers to this phenomenon as switch contention in their literature. Tree saturation [Kuma86] will not occur since the Butterfly interconnect is a non-blocking network. That is, the Butterfly switch forces uncompleted messages to retreat back to their source rather than buffer-up behind a blocked switch node. An alternate route is then tried for the message after some random delay time. The amount of time taken to serve a given request will increase as more messages enter the network since it may take longer to find a free path in this situation. In fact, if we distribute the dataset uniformly throughout the processor memories, this probability increases non-linearly as P is increased since the number of switch paths in the Butterfly grows as $log(P)$ while the number of processors grows linearly.

Network contention in the different algorithms is measured in the following manner. First, the time for task i is measured with P active processors (in this case, $P = 96$). Then, the time for task i is measured with only a single processor active, but using the memory of MIN processors (so no paging occurs). The time difference between the two scenarios is a result of contention in the P processor case, but no contention in the single processor case. Latency and/or communication costs are factored out of the times in each situation. Equation 4.10 shows the formula for computing network contention. The superscripted i refers to a particular task i.

$$\text{Switch Contention \%} = \frac{\sum\limits_{i=1}^{\#tasks} \left[T(P)^i - T(1)^i \right]}{T_p \bullet P} * 100 \%$$

(4.10)

Another form of contention which is more specific to a particular switch location is called *hot spot contention*. This occurs when a disproportionately large amount of references are aimed at either: 1) a particular memory location or 2) a particular switch node. The first situation can usually be rectified by copying this data item to all memory modules in the system except in situations in which the data item is writable where there would be no solution. This copying involves the use of the network which can contribute to other contention problems. The second situation is less easily identifiable, but scattering of the shared data structures uniformly throughout the network is the usual way to solve this problem. Both types of solutions are used when possible in the algorithms described in this book and no adverse effects due to hot spot contention were noticed.

4.3.2.7. Load Imbalance

Load balancing is the primary focus of most designers of parallel programs. It is usually desirable for all processors to finish working on a problem at the same time so that none are left idle while others are busy. This is almost impossible to achieve in general practice, though. The idle time delay in which processors wait until all tasks are finished is due to load imbalance. Any solution used to solve this problem should take into account the performance of the given machine with regard to scheduling time, its CPU speed, and of course parallel program decomposition.

In measuring the contribution of load imbalance in each algorithm, the finishing times of each processor are noted. The average of these finishing times is the theoretical ideal finishing time if load balancing is perfect. To calculate the percentage overhead, the difference in time between the last processor's finishing time and the average of all processors is recorded. This difference is used as the numerator for calculating the load imbalance percentage, as shown in equation 4.11. This is essentially the same as adding up the total idle time at the end of the computation for all processors in the system.

$$\text{Load Imbalance \%} = \frac{T_{max} \bullet P - T_{avg} \bullet P}{T_p \bullet P} * 100 \%$$

(4.11)

It is very difficult in reality to isolate how well a particular algorithm is load balanced. A problem with equation 4.11 is that it does not delete the effects of network contention. In fact, it may turn out that this overhead percentage is artificially increased or decreased in a situation where contention is significant. Although we cannot isolate how load balancing would be treated in each instance if contention is not present, the load balancing percentage determined by equation 4.11is a rough indication of this overhead factor. This allows direct comparisons to be made between the different algorithms by using a common measurement parameter.

4.4. Summary

In this chapter, we present the serial algorithm on which all of the parallel algorithms are based. A detailed description is provided of each of the important phases of the program, elaborating upon the data structures which are common to all the implementations in their use of shared memory. Information is given about the test scenes used for timing purposes. Next, methods describing performance analysis for the parallel programs are elaborated upon. The traditional performance measurements of time, speedup, and efficiency as well as other overhead factors are described.

In the next chapter, these additional overhead factors are quantitatively presented in an analysis of parallel graphics display algorithms to show where the performance degradation actually occurs. In addition, the different parallel partitioning schemes identified in chapter 2 were implemented on the Butterfly, and their results are presented. An analysis of their performance is included in regard to: the execution time of the tiling section, speedup, and effect of the overhead factors.

5

Comparison of Task Partitioning Schemes

In this chapter, we describe a number of parallel decomposition schemes and our implementations of these schemes on the BBN Butterfly GP1000. In these algorithms, tasks are assigned to regions of image space, but there are a number of different ways of determining the size and number of these regions. Task partitioning can be divided into two main techniques which are discussed in this chapter: data non-adaptive and data adaptive. In the data non-adaptive method, tasks are determined without regard to the input data set. In the data adaptive approach, the number and size of tasks are based on the input dataset. The data non-adaptive partitioning scheme relies on dynamic scheduling of tasks onto processors. These tasks are determined in a simple manner, so little overhead is needed prior to tiling. Load balancing is achieved by creating enough tasks so that the tasks left to work on at the end of the computation are fairly small. Data adaptive partitioning in a graphics context involves creating tasks based on the location of the data elements on the screen. The basic idea in this method is that tasks are chosen prior to tiling, so that each task takes approximately the same amount of time to finish. Extra work is required to set up these tasks prior to tiling but the benefit of this is reduced scheduling overhead. For each of these methods, one can assign a number of tasks equal to the number of processors ($T = P$) or greater than the number of processors ($T > P$). This is illustrated in figure 5.1. There is also an important extension to the data non-adaptive technique known as *task adaptive*.

Each section in this chapter describes a different task partitioning scheme in detail. The algorithm implementations which are discussed in chapter 2 are presented in detail here and categorized according to their task partitioning scheme. Each implementation is then evaluated according to the parallel program measurements of time and speedup. Then, the overhead factors of scheduling, memory latency, communication, network contention, load imbalance, overhead due to adaptation for parallel execution, and synchronization are quantified for each algorithm. The results from this analysis help form a basis for comparison of all of the implemented approaches. The values reported in this chapter pertain only to the tiling section of the parallel programs. In the next chapter, a comparative analysis of the operations required prior to tiling is included along with the time of the tiling section.

The various schemes are described in the following sections. We analyze the implementations with regard to the issues discussed in the previous chapters. The task partitioning schemes as discussed in this chapter are given in the following order: data non-adaptive approach, data adaptive approach, and task adaptive approach.

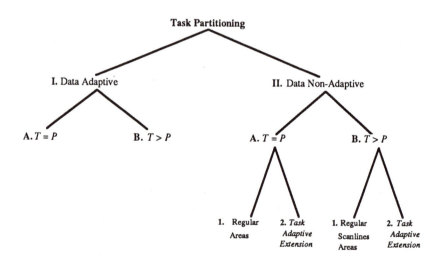

Figure 5.1: Task partitioning techniques

5.1. Data Non-Adaptive Partitioning Scheme

The data non-adaptive partitioning scheme relies on subdividing the image space regardless of the screen location of the polygon datasets. When this method is implemented under the Uniform System, it employs a dynamic scheduling mechanism whereby tasks are scheduled onto processors as each processor is available for work. Each task is a single region or area; a single scan line is a task in the first method, and a small rectangular region is a task in the second method. The granularity ratio, which is the ratio of total areas to the number of processors (R=#$tasks$/P), must be chosen carefully since it can have a significant impact on load imbalance and execution overheads. We will see how this value affects the overall performance in the decomposition schemes outlined below.

In this partitioning method, image space is broken up into a number of rectangular areas, all the same size. The two methods from chapter 2 which were implemented are Hu and Foley's dynamic scan line scheme and the rectangular area scheme suggested by Kaplan and Greenberg, as well as Whelan.

5.1.1. Scan line Decomposition

A scan line decomposition is probably the most natural parallel partitioning scheme. It was first suggested by Hu and Foley in their paper describing a hardware parallel rendering machine [Hu85]. The basic idea involves partitioning the image space such that each scan line is a task by itself (T=#$scan\ lines$). The granularity ratio R varies as P is increased since T is constant for all values of P. The algorithm has less flexibility than if T could be increased with P since load balancing is limited as this number is approached by P. Some details regarding the implementation of this decomposition in parallel are given here.

As in a serial scan line algorithm, a y-bucket list is used to store the polygons relevant to a particular scan line. Additional work is required in constructing the y-bucket data structure for a parallel implementation because *all* polygons relevant to that scan line are stored in a given y-bucket, not just those that start on a given scan line. The set of operations necessary to construct this shared data structure is performed in the front end prior to tiling. In reference to a conventional serial algorithm, extra memory is required for the y-bucket list in addition to the extra time necessary to store the data. These extra requirements are small when compared with the benefit gained through parallel processing.

The storage and access for the y-bucket list is accomplished in the following manner. Only one processor works on a given scan line, so no synchronization is necessary for extracting the polygons from this data structure. The y-bucket list is stored as an array corresponding to the number of scan lines, where each element of the array is a pointer to a linked list of the polygons relevant to that scan line (a single y-bucket). Since all processors need to reference this array of pointers, it is copied to each processor's local memory to avoid hot spot contention. Prior to tiling, the links for each scan line are loaded into the y-bucket data structure and scattered throughout the memory modules; thus there is only one copy of each link. This achieves a uniform distribution of the polygonal dataset, without adding contention. The y-bucket array is read-only in the tiling phase of the program, which is why it can be copied to all the processors. The links could also be copied, but the time to do so and the memory required make this inefficient.

Hu and Foley's research showed that dynamic assignment of single scan lines to processors resulted in better performance than interleaving groups of successive scan lines statically. The reason the dynamic technique was superior was that it minimized load imbalance, and this had a greater impact on performance than maximizing coherence in a group of contiguous scan lines. This dynamic assignment method was implemented and tested on the Butterfly to evaluate the algorithm on a real machine. A graph of the times for each of the test images is given in figure 5.2.

It is important to note that Hu and Foley achieved their results from simulation data rather than from an actual implementation. In addition, their design was intended for hardware implementation and required all the data to be present in each processor, while we are using a more flexible memory model in a software algorithm. Consequently, issues like remote memory referencing come into play in this implementation, whereas Hu and Foley did not analyze their algorithm with regard to these issues. The results given here compare favorably with their results, although different test cases were used and exact speedup was not recorded in their paper. The relative speedup for the images is shown in figure 5.3.

The equation to calculate speedup is known as *Amdahl's law* and is shown in equation 5.1 where P is the maximum number of processors used (in this case, $P = 96$). As we explained in the previous chapter, all the tests were started above one processor, so the actual speedup must be estimated. The estimated speedup is derived by using $T_{MIN}(1)$ in the numerator of equation 5.1. This value refers to the fact that the program is run on one processor using MIN memory modules with a deduction for the communication cost. This was shown in equation 4.3 in the previous chapter.

$$\text{Speedup} = \frac{T(1)}{T(P)}$$

(5.1)

We will now discuss the various issues associated with parallel computation, described in section 4.3.2 for this algorithm. As a guide to the reader, the range of percentage contributions for each overhead based on the minimum and maximum overhead of the four test images is included in parentheses after the section title. The overhead factors determined are based on the percentage of the processor-time space using the equations given in chapter 4. The appendix contains all of the results from the tests used to determine these overheads.

In the previous chapter, a description is given of how each overhead factor is actually measured. Due to the variance in the way each algorithm works, some changes in the way these overheads are measured is required. These changes are described as necessary here.

All of the tests were run on a maximum of 96 processors. Since this maximum value of P represents the worst case scenario in relation to the overhead factors, these factors are evaluated at $P = 96$.

5.1.1.1. Scheduling (0.002% - 0.01%)

Scheduling in the parallel scan line algorithm proceeds by calling a generator procedure which is provided by the Uniform System. It is equivalent to a parallel *for* loop based on the number of scan lines in the final image. Processors extract iterations from the generator as each processor is available to work on a task. The minimum time that it takes to render a scan line occurs when no polygons are present and only the background color is displayed. The average time to calculate background for a scan line of 640 pixels and then write the scan line to the virtual frame buffer is $T_{back} = 2.0$ msec.

As stated in section 4.3.2.1, the time to schedule the first task on each of the 96 processors is $96 * T_{crit}$ (the critical region time $T_{crit} = 24$ µsec) which is 2.3 msec and is denoted as T_{sched}. T_{sched} is the total serial scheduling time overhead. It is slightly larger than T_{back} (the background color rendering time), so it is possible to create a bottleneck if a very high proportion of the tasks to be executed are background tasks.

Parallel Scan line Algorithm Performance

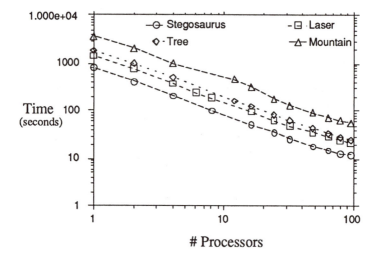

Figure 5.2: Scan line data non-adaptive performance

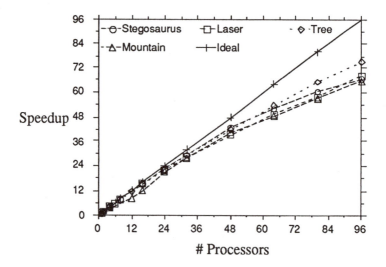

Figure 5.3: Speedup for scan line data non-adaptive algorithm

This bottleneck is unlikely to occur in practical use and would only degrade overall performance by a fraction of a millisecond if it should occur. Using equation 4.5, we plug in values of $P = 96$, $N = 484$, and $T_{crit} = 24$ μsec as shown in equation 5.2. Note that $(P * (P - 1))/2$ can be substituted for the summation in equation 4.5. T_p is the parallel execution time on 96 processors for each image.

$$\text{Scheduling \%} = \frac{\dfrac{(95 \bullet 96)}{2} \bullet 24 \text{ μsec} + (484 - 96) \bullet 24 \text{ μsec}}{T_p \bullet 96} \tag{5.2}$$

The overhead due to scheduling in the parallel scan line algorithm ranges from 0.002% for the mountain image to 0.01% for the stegosaurus image.

5.1.1.2. Memory Latency (3.0% - 5.6%)

Recall that memory latency is the additional time delay incurred when a reference is made to a remote rather than a local memory module. The latency is calculated using equation 4.6, by using the total number of remote references during the computation to determine the extra time spent in accessing non-local data.

We have calculated the latency overhead percentage for the parallel scan line algorithm at 96 processors for the various images to be a minimum of 3.0% for the stegosaurus image and up to the maximum of 5.6% for the mountain image. Although it might be expected that the larger datasets require more remote references, it is interesting to note that the percentage overhead due to latency also increases with dataset size. In other words, even though the larger datasets require more execution time, the latency requires an even greater percentage of this time. This suggests that latency might become a major degradation factor for particularly large input datasets.

5.1.1.3. Network Contention (8.9% - 23.1%)

Network contention is a function of the probability that a conflict will occur in the interconnection network for a particular memory reference. As P is increased, the likelihood of a blocked network path increases since the number of remote references is proportional to P^2 while the number of switch paths only increases by $P \bullet \log(P)$. In the appendix, the network contention is quoted as two percentage values. The first value, denoted "% of Total-Processor Time Space," is measured using equation 4.10, as given in the previous chapter. The second value is calculated as described next.

We assume that the measurements used for load imbalance, memory latency, communication, code modification, and scheduling are all somewhat accurate. This is a reasonable assumption since with the exception of load imbalance, all of these overheads can be measured independently from the others. Load balancing is affected by all of the overhead values, but this cannot be avoided in normal timings or in specialized performance measurement situations. The value given for load imbalance is probably a culmination of other factors as well. Network contention is a completely separate matter. Although the measurement technique used for this culprit should be somewhat indicative of the effect of this overhead, the method given in chapter 4 does not involve a true measurement of the actual network contention. Doing so would require hardware monitoring which can only be done by the manufacturer. Therefore, the assumption given above is used to help estimate the actual network contention. This is done by subtracting the sequential time and overheads, which are assumed to be accurate from the total processor-time space, as is shown in equation 5.3.

$$\text{Contention} = T_p \bullet P - \left[\begin{array}{l} T_{MIN}(1) + \text{Code Mod.} + \text{Latency/Comm.} + \\ \text{Load Imbal.} + \text{Synch.} + \text{Sched.} \end{array} \right] \quad (5.3)$$

In other words, we assume that the total of the sequential time plus all overhead factors is exactly the parallel execution time. Therefore, if all other overheads are deemed to be accurately measured, then the only overhead left is contention. In most cases, our measured value of contention using equation 4.10 and the calculated value of contention did not differ by a large amount, meaning that the measurement technique is fairly reasonable. This can be seen in the values given in the appendix. This calculated value for contention is given in the header of this subsection and the other algorithms' subsections as well.

Since this algorithm requires a large amount of remote references, as shown above, it is likely that the contention is fairly high as well. The results from the tests bear this out. Based on the scan line algorithm overhead measurements, the calculated network contention ranges from 8.9% for the tree image to 23.1% for the stegosaurus image.

5.1.1.4. Load Imbalance (6.8% - 10.4%)

It is hard to obtain good load balancing in this task partitioning scheme since the number of processors comes close to the number of total tasks. In this case, 96 processors and 484 scan lines provide approximately a 5 to 1 ratio of tasks to processors. Since it is entirely possible that any given task will take more than 5 times longer than another task, it is possible that load balancing will not be adequate with this number of tasks. For 96 processors, the load imbalance for the test images has been measured from 6.8% for the mountain image to 10.4% for the laser image.

5.1.1.5. Code Modification (4.9% - 9.8%)

Overhead due to parallel processing is fairly significant in this algorithm. The main contributor to the overhead in this rendering algorithm is the loss of coherence incurred by starting a new scan line in parallel rather than continuing execution on the same processor. While this factor is constant (since the number of tasks is constant regardless of the number of processors used) and will not affect the speedup of the parallel algorithm, it can be used to determine the relative performance of this algorithm versus the other parallel algorithms. The overall percentage effect due to code modification varies from 4.9% for the tree image to 9.8% for the mountain image.

5.1.1.6. Explanation of Results

The two primary contributors to performance degradation in this algorithm include overhead due to code modification and network contention. Memory latency and load imbalance also degrade overall performance, although to a lesser degree. The percentages for each of the major overhead factors as related to each test image are given in figure 5.4. The effects of scheduling are so minimal in comparison to the other factors that it is not worth consideration as a problem area here.

Recall from the previous chapter that the dataset sizes are as follows:

1. Stegosaurus	9.7K polygons
2. Laser	46.3K polygons
3. Tree	106.4K polygons
4. Mountain	131.1K polygons

As one can see from the figure, latency increases with dataset size. The overhead measured for load imbalance is stable, although it is reduced slightly for the mountain image. Since the mountain data is more uniformly spread across the screen, this may be the reason that load balancing is better for this image than the others.

It seems remarkable that even with an average of only 5 tasks per processor using test cases in which the data is not uniformly distributed, the load imbalance is less than 10% for most of the test images. It is certainly true, however, that if the number of processors were to be increased significantly beyond 96, load balancing would suffer due to a reduction in the number of tasks available for parallel execution. This provides a motivation to seek algorithms which are better able to handle large processor configurations as well as variable size resolution images.

Lack of vertical scan line coherence is the primary contributor to the overhead in adapting this algorithm for parallel processing. This is manifest as the total degradation due to code modification. The code modification overhead is less than 10% for all the test images. The actual time due to code modification is invariant to the number of processors in the system. Unfortunately, as P is increased significantly, load balancing tends to suffer to a large degree in this algorithm. A better algorithmic solution would be one which does not have this overhead effect.

Network contention is a major contributor to performance degradation, and it increases as a function of the number of

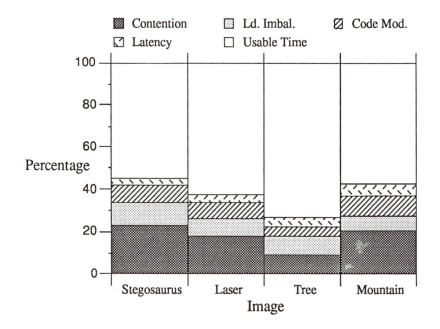

Figure 5.4: Degradation factors for scan line decomposition for ($P = 96$)

processors. The key to solving this problem is to reduce the number of remote memory requests. As we mentioned previously, it is likely that remote references became blocked in the switch since the tasks assigned to processors involved adjacent scan lines. If the scan lines were assigned in some haphazard order, this effect might be alleviated since the data to be referenced would not be the same. On the other hand, with a large number of processors such as 96, it probably could not be reduced significantly. The dataset size could also impact the network contention since larger datasets require more references. The combination of these two factors seems to indicate that this overhead cannot be reduced in the general case unless a radical change in the memory referencing scheme is applied. If coherence can be maximized without sacrificing load balancing and can still maintain adequate parallelism, some of these factors can be reduced significantly. The algorithm described in the next section is a logical extension of this one and attempts to achieve these goals.

5.1.2. Rectangular Region Decomposition (UD Scheme)

The rectangular region decomposition algorithm is a generalization of the scan line decomposition algorithm. Instead of using single scan lines as wide as the screen for each task, a small group of contiguous scan lines is designated as a single task.[1] This idea was first suggested by Kaplan and Greenberg [Kapl79], where they implemented both the Watkins and the Warnock algorithm [Roge85] as two alternative rectangular approaches. In their Warnock implementation, equal size areas are initially assigned to all processors. The Warnock cull was then used within each single task.

5.1.2.1. Coherence Effect on Rectangular Regions

Presumably, the reason the Warnock algorithm was chosen for a rectangular area partition is due to the area coherence exploited in this algorithm. In the case here, however, a scan line Z-buffer is the basis algorithm for each single area task since this algorithm is inherently faster than Warnock's. Kaplan and Greenberg chose full scan line width tasks (of multiple contiguous scan lines) for their Watkins approach. The probable reason for this was to capitalize on

---

[1]As a reference note, from now on, when we refer to "scan lines" in the context of an algorithm such as this, we mean a scan line within the width of the area.

the vertical span coherence exploited by that algorithm. Hu and Foley showed that this type of contiguous approach did not provide sufficient load balancing in comparison to the dynamic single scan line method presented in the previous subsection. Since a scan line Z-buffer is used here and not a Watkins spanning scan line algorithm as a sequential task basis, there are no spans to update in the vertical dimension. Therefore, the aspect ratio (their width versus height) of the rectangular areas chosen as single tasks is open to further analysis. The type of coherence lost when a region is started anew is in the vertical direction. For the first scan line of a region, all of the polygons which started above the area but are still relevant to it need to be initialized. Figure 5.5 illustrates those polygons.

This initialization is not necessary if vertical coherence is maintained. On the other hand, some initialization is required for polygons which have their top vertex in the region to the immediate left or right of the current region as well. This initialization is also unnecessary if horizontal coherence is maintained.

Another loss due to coherence in the horizontal direction is the update of edge interpolation parameters for those edges which intersect the region adjacent to the current one on its left. A multiply and an add operation are required for each interpolation parameter update, whereas an add operation is all that is needed if horizontal coherence is maintained. Note that all of these factors would change if clipping is implemented at the region level, but this is not done in the implementations described here. The losses due to coherence are further illustrated in figure 5.6.

For the purposes of this discussion, it is assumed that for a particular polygon and a square region, the loss in time due to horizontal

Polygons relevant to first scanline
of the area

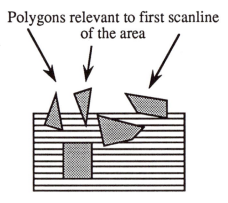

Figure 5.5: Polygons relevant to an area but starting above it

coherence and vertical coherence is nearly the same. In the vertical case, the initialization overhead is fairly costly and occurs for all polygons above the area but relevant to it. The horizontal initialization cost is only valid for polygons whose top vertex enters the left or right adjacent regions (not counting screen boundaries since clipping occurs there). The other horizontal coherence loss at the scan line level is small in comparison since it only involves the left adjacent region and is of complexity $O(e * h * T_{mult})$ where e is the number of edges in the left region and the current region, h is the height of each of these edges in the left region portion, and T_{mult} is the time for a multiply instruction. In any case, because of the wide variation in polygon size and number in currently used imagery, it appears that any inaccuracy encountered by invalidity of these assumptions would be minor.

5.1.2.2. Aspect Ratio Choice

From figure 5.6 it can be seen that coherence is lost only along the perimeter of the region, particularly along the left and top sides. If the regions are tall and narrow, horizontal coherence is completely lost, but little vertical coherence is lost, as is shown in figure 5.7. The opposite is true for wide regions, as shown in figure 5.8. For nearly square regions, some degree of coherence is lost in both directions as shown in figure 5.9. The total perimeter of a rectangular region is a function of its aspect ratio and is shown in equation 5.4, where b is the length of the base and h is the height.

$$\text{perimeter} = 2 \bullet (b + h) \qquad (5.4)$$

Thus, if the aspect ratio of a given region is 1:3, the perimeter is 2 $\bullet$ $(1 + 3)$ $\bullet$ x, or on the order of $8x$. If the aspect ratio is 1:1, the

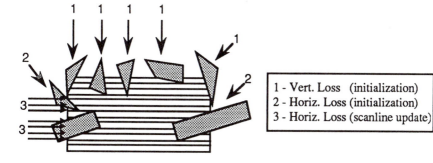

Figure 5.6: Loss due to coherence in vertical and horizontal directions

perimeter is $2 \cdot (1 + 1) \cdot x$ or $4x$. It therefore seems logical that the situation which results in the least perimeter for regions will also have the least loss due to coherence. A few simple tests were done on a test image of nearly uniform polygon distribution across the scene to verify these assertions. The results are given in table 5.1.

Table 5.1: Aspect ratio (width:height) time comparison in seconds

Ratio	3:1	2:1	1:1	1:2	1:3
Time	25.8	22.7	21.8	21.9	33.6

Based on the analysis and the experimental data, it seems like a 1:1 aspect ratio is the most suitable choice for high performance for a rectangular region decomposition. This verifies Whelan's experimental tests in which he compared vertical, horizontal, and rectangular decompositions. This method is illustrated in figure 5.9 and also in color plate 2. The same shared memory referencing method is used here as in the previous algorithm, namely the uniformly distributed (UD) scheme.

5.1.2.3. Granularity Ratio Comparison

This algorithm requires a methodology to determine the granularity ratio R to be used for a given image or given number of processors (recall that $R = \#tasks/P$). It seems clear that a ratio of $R = 1$ would not produce adequate load balancing for images which contain data that is not uniformly distributed across the scene. Some questions need to be answered in order to determine what this ratio should be, and if it should change depending on the image or number of processors. Other researchers in the past (notably Fuchs and Johnson [Fuch79]) have used static assignment of tasks onto processors in an attempt to develop an evenly load balanced system. While static assignment may be preferable in some instances, it is not necessary since the Uniform System on the Butterfly uses a small amount of overhead in implementing a dynamic scheduler. In the algorithm used here, a large number of tasks which are easily determined are executed in a dynamic fashion.

The dynamic method reduces load imbalance, and since the tasks are small at the end of the computation, very little work is left to perform. The number of tasks created strongly influences the degree of success of the load balancing.

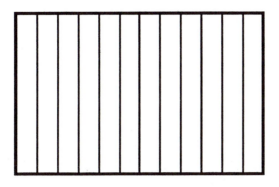

Figure 5.7: Vertical subdivision

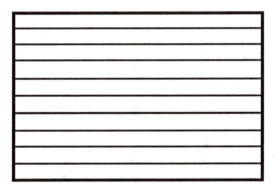

Figure 5.8: Horizontal subdivision

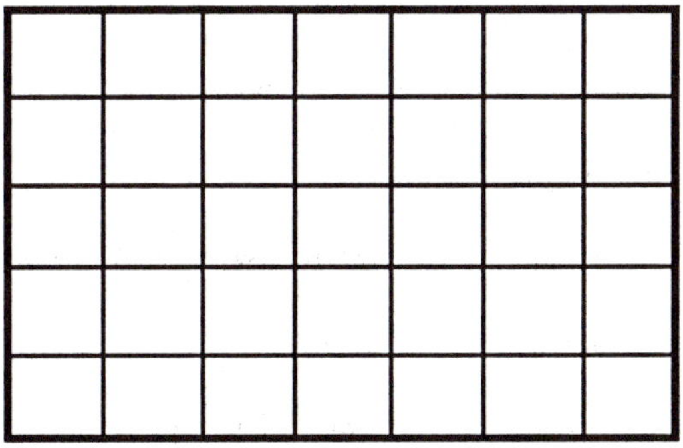

Figure 5.9: Rectangular mesh subdivision

On the other hand, if too many tasks are assigned, load imbalance is reduced, but the overhead of assigning more tasks will introduce additional loss of coherence, communication, and network contention. Therefore, to choose the appropriate granularity ratio for a particular combination of (image, #processors), a series of experiments was designed to evaluate the performance of a particular granularity ratio R. These are shown in figures A.1, A.2, A.3, and A.4 in the appendix. The data for the mountain image is given in figure 5.10 as a representative example. From the graphs, it seems clear that ratios anywhere in the range from 16 to 1 up to 28 to 1 are suitable for most of the imagery. A compromise ratio of 24 to 1 was decided as the single choice to be used in the main timing experiments.

One important note here is that the value of R determined above was evaluated on 96 processors since this was the maximum number of processors used. Due to increases in communication and network contention as the number of processors increases, this value of R may be higher than desirable if more processors are to be used. Either educated guesses or empirical testing similar to above would be required for a given processor configuration, especially if a different machine architecture were to be used. It is not reasonable to attempt to determine this ratio mathematically a priori since the overhead factors are too hard to predict for a given image. The times for all

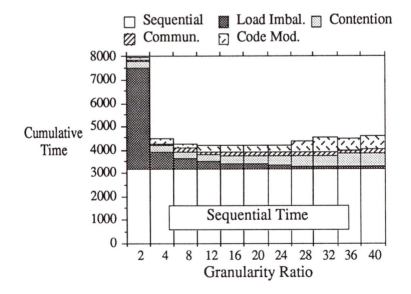

Figure 5.10: Granularity ratio comparison for mountain image, UD scheme

images using $R = 24$ and a 1:1 image aspect ratio for the regions are shown in figure 5.11. The speedup graph can be seen in figure 5.12. Although an aspect ratio of 1:1 for the regions was desired for all values of P, this could not be achieved for each combination of R and P. Therefore, an aspect ratio as close to 1:1 was used when needed (all regions have the same aspect ratio for a given value of P).

We will now analyze this algorithm with regard to the issues identified previously to determine the various overhead percentages.

5.1.2.4. Scheduling (0.004% - 0.013%)

In this decomposition method, it is necessary to schedule all regions as separate tasks, but the number of regions varies as the number of processors is increased. To determine the maximum number of regions to be scheduled, we used the granularity ratio (R) of 24 to 1 on 96 processors, which results in a total of 2,304 tasks to schedule. The time to run a task consisting solely of the background color for one of these areas has been measured as $T_{back} = 2.3$ msec. The reason this is larger than in the scan line decomposition case is that a separate block transfer is necessary for each scan line in the area and each block transfer requires a setup cost. Since 2.3 msec is exactly the overhead time to schedule 96 tasks on 96 processors (T_{sched}), scheduling will not become a bottleneck in this algorithm. The overhead due to scheduling then involves plugging the values for this algorithm into equation 4.5, as shown below. This time represents a percentage overhead for the different images, ranging from 0.004% for the mountain image to 0.013% for the stegosaurus image.

$$\text{Scheduling \%} = \frac{\dfrac{(95 \bullet 96)}{2} \bullet 24 \text{ } \mu\text{sec} + (2{,}304 - 96) \bullet 24 \text{ } \mu\text{sec}}{T_p \bullet 96} \bullet 100 \text{ \%}$$

(5.5)

5.1.2.5. Memory Latency (1.4% - 3.6%)

In this algorithm, memory latency is measured the same way as the previous method, namely by counting the number of remote references and using equation 4.6 to determine the overall percentage. Fewer references to the shared data are needed than in the previous approach due to the coherence maintained within a region. Consequently, the overall latency is reduced.

Rectangular Region Algorithm (UD Scheme) Performance

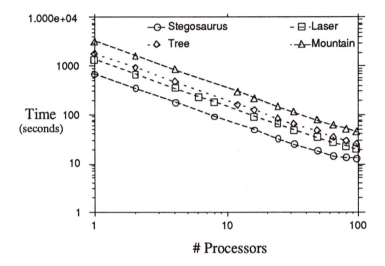

Figure 5.11: Rectangular region performance (UD scheme)

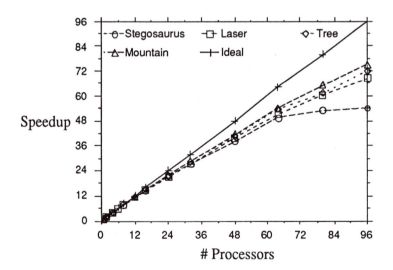

Figure 5.12: Speedup of rectangular region decomposition (UD scheme)

The percentage time of latency for this algorithm for the different test images ranges from 1.4% for the stegosaurus image to 3.6% for the mountain image. The latency increases corresponding to an increase in dataset size, which is the same phenomenon observed previously.

Most remote references occur for the first scan line of a region since it is necessary to retrieve the data from remote memory and store it in local data structures. Once this is accomplished, the majority of references are local, with the exception being a small amount of remote referencing required in the anti-aliasing portion of the code (this would be the same for each of these algorithms). The remote referencing in the anti-aliasing section stems from the need to obtain the plane equation for each polygon for stochastic sampling purposes. Since the previous algorithm incorporates no vertical scan line coherence, all the data for each scan line must be referenced remotely. The rectangular region partitioning scheme capitalizes on coherence within the region so that remote referencing is reduced.

5.1.2.6. Network Contention (5.6% - 33.1%)

The network contention is calculated in the same manner for this algorithm as it was for the last one. Using this technique, the percentage effect of network contention for the various test images varies from 5.6% for the tree image to 33.1% for the stegosaurus image.

The contention in this algorithm as compared to the parallel scan line approach is worse for the stegosaurus and Laser images, but improved for the tree and mountain images. It is difficult to speculate as to the reason for this without further image analysis. Regardless, one can see that even with a reduced number of references (as compared to the parallel scan line approach), contention is still a major degradation factor. Most of the increase in network contention occurs as the number of processors is increased from 64 to 96 processors, indicating that the switch network becomes overloaded with requests somewhere in this range.

5.1.2.7. Load Imbalance (4.3% - 11.5%)

The granularity ratio in this algorithm provides a better load balanced system than the last algorithm, although network contention increases the execution time and this varies the overall finishing times. The load imbalance percentages measured at 96 processors for the different images varies from 4.3% for the mountain image to 11.5% for the tree image. When compared to the previous algorithm, the load imbalance overhead is less for this algorithm, with the exception of the tree test image. The granularity ratio comparison in figure A.3 for this image indicates that load balancing is not particularly good at any value of R and in fact gets worse after $R = 24$.

In general, though, this algorithm yields better load balancing than the scan line approach since the granularity ratio provides enough tasks to minimize the load imbalance over a wide range of processor configurations.

5.1.2.8. Code Modification (7.9% - 9.6%)

This algorithm has a different amount of coherence overhead than the scan line algorithm since rectangular regions are generated as tasks. Due to the rectangular nature of the regions, coherence is taken advantage of in both the vertical and horizontal directions within a single task. On the other hand, the lack of vertical scan line coherence at the beginning of an area results in extra work required to start the first scan line of a region. In addition, the lack of horizontal coherence at the boundary to the left causes an overhead of interpolating parameters for polygons which extend beyond this boundary.

The code modification overhead is measured the same as before using equation 4.8. Based on the measured values, the overhead percentages vary from 7.9% for the mountain image to 9.6% for the tree image. Considering the fact that there are many more tasks used in this scheme versus the parallel scan line approach (2,304 vs. 484), this overhead factor does not seem out of line in comparison.

5.1.2.9. Explanation of Results

The rectangular region decomposition scheme achieves reduced overheads primarily in memory latency and to some degree in network contention and load balancing, in comparison to the parallel scan line algorithm. The reduction in latency is due to the fact that most remote referencing occurs for the first scan line of an area, and this effect is reduced in the rectangular region algorithm. This suggests that the rectangular region decomposition algorithm will perform better than the scan line algorithm in the general case due to its performance advantages in the tests given. The scan line algorithm exhibits poor scalability as P is increased since load balancing will suffer as the number of scan lines approach the number of processors. The rectangular region algorithm uses a fixed granularity ratio which allows better load balancing as the number of processors is increased; thus its scalability is superior to the parallel scan line approach.

It is important to note that this algorithm still has its share of problems. Network contention still represents a significant overhead. The code modification overhead is not reduced in this algorithm in comparison to the scan line approach. A comparison of the major degradation factors is given in figure 5.13.

Since the number of remote references is reduced in this algorithm but contention was not significantly reduced, another tactic is necessary to solve this problem. Consequently, it is necessary to implement a different memory referencing scheme that is designed to reduce the network contention noted in parallel implementations. This memory referencing strategy is referred to as the locally cached (LC) scheme and is described in the next section.

5.1.3. Rectangular Region Decomposition (LC Scheme)

The algorithm described here is implemented exactly the same as the last one, with the only exception being the remote memory referencing strategy. A brief description of this strategy, denoted the Locally Cached or LC scheme, follows. Instead of referencing globally

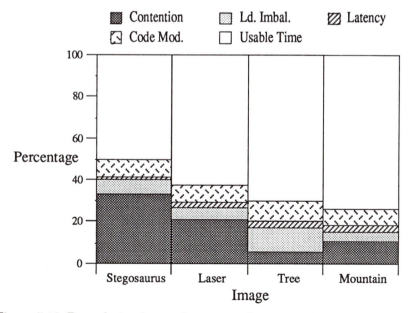

Figure 5.13: Degradation factors for rectangular region decomposition, (UD Scheme, $P = 96$)

shared data remotely, the data is cached into the local memory module prior to referencing, thus allowing it to be accessible quickly. Although others have used an elaborate software caching mechanism for computer graphics rendering ([Gree89] and [Bado90]), we rely on the fact that the exact data needed for a given task can be copied directly to each processor prior to the computation of a given region. If a data element is relevant to more than one processor, it is copied to all processors which would reference it, incurring a space penalty. The extra memory required due to duplication is shown in the appendix in figures A.9, A.10, A.11, and A.12. These figures show the duplication of data by copying data elements as a function of the total number of regions. Although the extra memory required is wasteful, a tradeoff of space versus time is necessary to achieve faster memory referencing than the previous Uniformly Distributed (UD) approach. The cost of non-local memory access is eliminated by block transferring data from its global storage location to the local memory of the processor(s) that need it. Details of the LC scheme are given in chapter 6.

5.1.3.1. Granularity Ratio

The granularity ratio R was re-evaluated for this algorithm to see what a good ratio would be, since a different memory referencing scheme is used. This ratio was tested at values of 2, 4, 8, 12, 16, 20, 24, 28, 32, 36, and 40 using the maximum configuration of 96 processors. Figure 5.14 shows the comparison for the Laser image as an example. In the appendix, figures A.5, A.6, A.7, and A.8 show the data for all the images. The downward slope of the curves is primarily due to a reduction in load imbalance as a higher granularity ratio is used. Then the curves continue upwards after a point since the other culprits introduce more overhead cost for the higher ratios. The minimum point on the curve is the optimal granularity ratio (R) to use for a particular scene. Each scene exhibits different characteristics which affect the choice of this optimal R so a compromise must be made so that a single value of R may be used in the general case.

In this case, the choice of a good ratio spans a broader range than in the UD scheme. The reason for this is the reduction in communication and contention costs versus the previous method. It seems like a good choice for R can be anywhere in the range from 12 to 1 up to 32 to 1. Since $R = 24$ was chosen for the previous algorithm and the performance for that ratio with this scheme is nearly optimal in most cases, this value will again be used. This ratio should provide good results for most imagery, given this machine configuration. Graphs for the time and speedup of this algorithm with the LC memory referencing scheme are given in figures 5.15 and 5.16.

The overhead factors for the rectangular region decomposition are now discussed, using the LC memory referencing scheme evaluated at 96 processors.

5.1.3.2. Scheduling (0.004% - 0.017%)

The time to run a background task (T_{back}) in this scheme is the same time as the previous one, since the only difference between the two is the memory referencing, which does not affect the background task. This algorithm is faster than the previous one, so the overhead percentage is slightly higher. Equation 5.5 is again used for evaluating the overhead due to scheduling for this algorithm. Based on this equation, the overhead due to scheduling varied from 0.004% overhead for the mountain image to 0.017% overhead for the stegosaurus image.

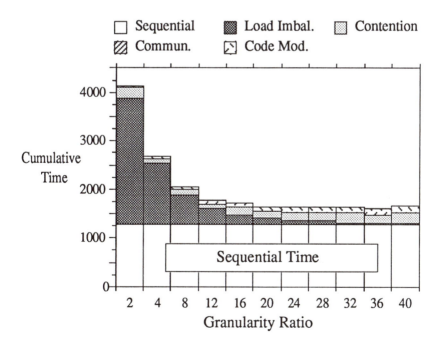

Figure 5.14: Comparison of ratios for Laser image

Rectangular Region Algorithm (LC Scheme) Performance

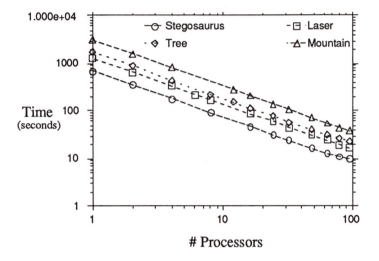

Figure 5.15: Tiling time for rectangular region partitioning (LC)

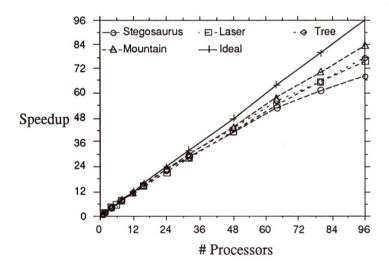

Figure 5.16: Speedup for rectangular region partitioning (LC Scheme)

5.1.3.3. Communication Overhead (0.03% - 0.05%)

Instead of latency due to remote referencing as in the UD case, communication occurs in blocks in this algorithm, resulting in a different overhead factor. This communication overhead is not present in the UD referencing method. Recall that this overhead is measured by a count of the total number of bytes transferred in the system during the computation. Using equation 4.7 given in the previous chapter, the communication overhead range is 0.03% for the stegosaurus image up to 0.05% for the mountain image. One can see that these values represent a significant drop in the amount of time necessary to transfer data in the system. Since the data is copied into local memory, all future references occur locally. This means that the total amount of data transferred is also reduced in comparison to the UD referencing scheme.

5.1.3.4. Network Contention (3.1% - 16.3%)

Although there is some overhead necessary to set up the blocks of data to be transferred in this algorithm, the deficit is more than made up for by a reduction in network contention when compared to the UD scheme. The calculated network contention overhead varies from 3.1% for the tree image to 16.3% for the stegosaurus image. The contention in this scheme is significantly less than in the previous one. This indicates that the locally cached memory referencing scheme does in fact reduce the messages in the system, which results in reduced chances for a blocked switch node.

5.1.3.5. Load Imbalance (4.5% - 11.1%)

The load imbalance in this algorithm is measured the same as before, using equation 4.11. The overhead percentages for load imbalance vary from 4.5% for the mountain image to 11.1% for the tree image. These values are nearly the same as those from the previous algorithm, which is to be expected since they both use the same partitioning method.

5.1.3.6. Code Modification (5.4% - 6.4%)

The code modification overhead using the LC scheme is less than in the UD scheme in all cases except the tree image. The measured overhead ranges from 5.4% for the mountain image to 6.4% for the stegosaurus image. The probable reason for the difference is that communication is not completely factored out of the measurement method. Recall that the measurement technique used for this overhead involves timing the program running on a single processor, using MIN memory modules. The UD scheme involves remote referencing to these memory modules, while the LC scheme does not. Although the communication cost is factored out of the measured time by counting the number of remote references or bytes transferred respectively, it is impossible to factor out the system overheads. Since the LC scheme will not likely include these to the degree that the UD scheme does due to the method of memory allocation and deallocation, the resultant code modification is a generally lower figure here.

5.1.3.7. Explanation of Results

Latency is no longer a factor using this memory referencing scheme, and although communication overhead is introduced, it is minimal. The change in memory referencing scheme also affects the overall code modification, as reported above.

The load imbalance is nearly the same as the previous algorithm, with the slight difference due to the effect of reduced contention in this algorithm. The chart in figure 5.17 indicates the overheads for the various images.

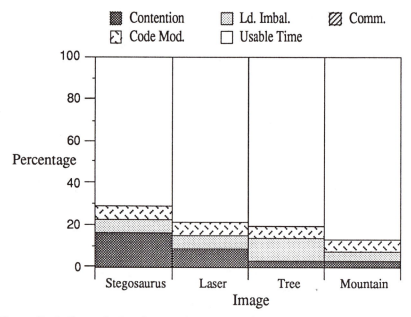

Figure 5.17: Degradation factors for rectangular region decomposition (LC Scheme, $P = 96$)

As one can see from the chart, network contention is still a problem, although it is significantly reduced in comparison to the UD scheme, especially for the more complex imagery. Load imbalance is also a problem, although the algorithm should scale up fairly well, especially when one takes into account the reduced contention using this memory reference strategy.

In the next section, we introduce another partitioning scheme which achieves even better load balancing.

5.2. Data Adaptive Partitioning Scheme

In a data adaptive algorithm, load balancing is achieved by constructing tasks which are estimated to take nearly the same amount of time. By using image space partitioning in a parallel graphics rendering program, tasks can be determined based on the location of data within the image. If the task work can be accurately predicted by using a heuristic, then the granularity ratio R can be reduced, resulting in less communication and scheduling. In fact, if the adaptation can produce exactly the same size tasks in terms of work, R can be reduced to 1. It is not generally possible to pick a very accurate heuristic since factors such as depth complexity, polygon area, and anti-aliasing all affect the time it takes to render a pixel. Pre-processing of the data cannot take all of these factors into account; otherwise it would require too much time. Following is a brief description of several algorithms which fall under the data adaptive category.

Whelan [Whel85] uses a data adaptive approach in his Median Cut algorithm, although his application was for a hardware architecture. His primary motivation was to reduce the scheduling overhead associated with the type of dynamic task assignment used in the algorithms discussed thus far. This is not necessary in a software multiprocessor approach since the Uniform System provides scheduling with a very small overhead. Whelan's approach involves task partitioning so that each task contains the same number of polygons. He uses the centroids of the polygons to determine their screen space location; however, extensive sorting is necessary to determine the locations to place the screen space partitions. His algorithm provides excellent load balancing, but the overhead cost of creating the areas outweighs the benefit of adaptive partitioning.

Roble's [Robl88] approach is another data adaptive method which also uses polygon location as a heuristic for determining tasks. His approach involves a large amount of communication prior to the tiling phase, and thus exhibits too much overhead as well.

Although there are many different decomposition methods that fall under the data adaptive method, one algorithm was chosen as a representative example for implementation. The goal here was to eliminate the excess overhead associated with this type of approach. This algorithm is described next.

5.2.1. Top-down Decomposition

A partitioning scheme similar to Whelan's Median Cut algorithm is used which takes comparatively less time to determine the task partitions. This scheme is based solely on the number of data elements in a region, regardless of the location of their centroids. The heuristic in this algorithm is based on the assumption that the number of polygons in a region is linearly related to the time it takes to tile that region. Using this simple heuristic, good load balancing can be achieved with a small overhead. The LC memory referencing scheme is used in the implementation of this algorithm based on the results shown in the previous section. The implementation is described below.

A 2D mesh is created as in the rectangular region decomposition, but this time the mesh is 4 times as dense (i.e. $\#regions = R \bullet P \bullet 4$). Polygons are placed into the mesh during the front end portion of the program as before, based on their screen space bounding boxes. Prior to tiling, adjacent meshes are combined hierarchically and a sum of the combined regions is stored in a tree data structure. This process is repeated until a point is reached where the entire screen is in a single region. Then, a data structure is created which consists of a hierarchical binary tree of counts referring to the number of data elements in each area.

After the tree is created, it is traversed in top-down fashion and the area with the most polygons at a given point is then split into its two components. This process is repeated by considering all areas created thus far, splitting the one with the next most polygons. The splitting process is stopped when the desired number of tasks has been reached. A count of the number of polygons in each small area is used, so it is not necessary to sequentially go through the entire list of potential polygons to determine which polygons are relevant to each area at this time. The limiting factor in the splitting is the leaf level, which is why a fairly dense mesh is created at the beginning. An example of this type of decomposition is illustrated graphically in figure 5.18 and also in color plate 3.

After the tree has been traversed, each of the regions is available for rendering in parallel. Some computational overhead exists for this scheme prior to the tiling phase, but fewer tasks are created than in the previous rectangular region approach. Figure 5.19 shows the performance for the various images using the data adaptive approach, with a value of $R = 10$. This value of R was determined empirically similar to the methods used previously. It is less than the value needed for the rectangular region scheme for good load balancing. A perfect match would result in a ratio of $R = 1$ but that situation is almost impossible to achieve using a heuristic which has minimal overhead cost. The relative speedup for the top-down scheme is shown in figure 5.20.

The time to build the tree data structure is not included in these timings since it is not part of the tiling section of the program. This time is fairly small anyway, but it is included in the overall algorithm comparison presented in chapter 6. We now analyze the top-down decomposition method with regard to the possible overhead factors.

5.2.1.1. Scheduling (0.003% - 0.01%)

This partitioning scheme uses regions that are not the same size, so each background task does not take the same time. The areas consist of groups of scan lines as before, but the number of scan lines and their size differ.

The average time to render the different background areas was measured for the different images. The results were fairly consistent, with an average background task time of 4.48 msec.

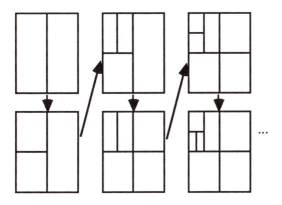

Figure 5.18: Top-down partitioning scheme

Top-down Algorithm (LC Scheme) Performance

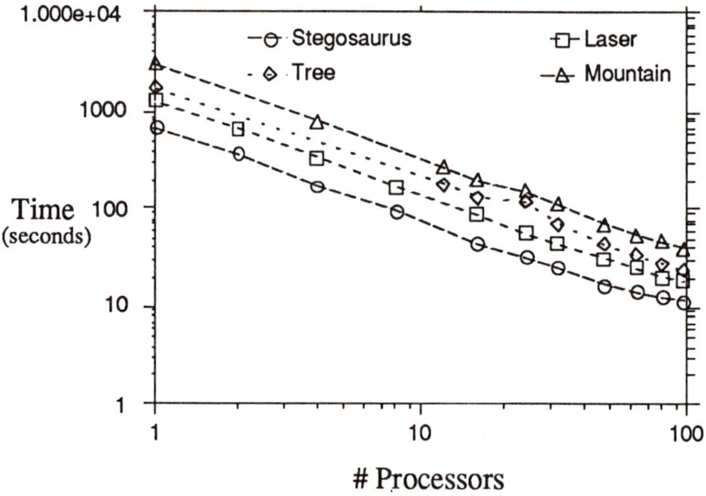

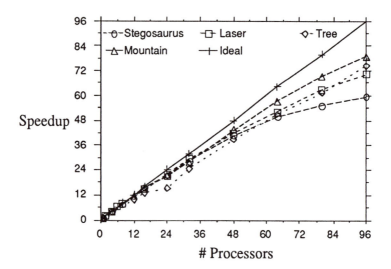

Figure 5.19: Top-down decomposition performance

Figure 5.20: Speedup of top-down decomposition method

This is more than T_{sched} (2.3 msec), which is the time it takes to schedule 96 tasks, so no bottleneck will occur due to scheduling. As before, the scheduling overhead is determined by plugging the values for this algorithm into equation 4.5, as shown in equation 5.6. Using this equation for 96 processors, the scheduling overhead for the test images ranges from 0.003% for the mountain image to 0.01% for the stegosaurus image.

$$\text{Scheduling \%} = \frac{\dfrac{(95 \bullet 96)}{2} \bullet 24 \ \mu sec + (960 - 96) \bullet 24 \ \mu sec}{T_p \bullet 96} \bullet 100 \ \% \tag{5.6}$$

5.2.1.2. Communication Overhead (0.02% - 0.04%)

The communication overhead is measured the same way as in the previous algorithm, by determining the number of bytes transferred in the system and using equation 4.7 to calculate the overhead. The values vary from 0.02% for the stegosaurus image to 0.04% for the mountain image. The communication overhead percentage in this algorithm is slightly less than in the rectangular region (LC) method since there are fewer areas.

5.2.1.3. Network Contention (11.8% - 34.9%)

Unfortunately, network contention is a significant factor in this algorithm, even more so than in the previous one. The network contention overhead ranges from 11.8% for the mountain image to 34.9% for the stegosaurus image. The reason for this increase in network contention is given here.

As was explained at the beginning of this section, a 2D dense mesh is created, from which small regions are clustered together to form tasks. The LC scheme requires communication from each of these small regions which form the larger clusters in order to obtain the data necessary for rendering a particular task area. Figure 5.21 illustrates this situation.

In order to render the cluster composed of sub-regions 1, 2, 3, and 4, it is necessary to retrieve the polygons from these sub-regions. This requires a block transfer from each of the sub-regions, whereas the rectangular region algorithm requires only one block transfer for the entire region. There may be even more than four sub-regions which are part of a larger cluster. Although the total amount of data is not large (evident by the communication factor given previously), the number of messages is higher than in the rectangular region algorithm due to this copying from sub-regions. In addition, the frequency of these communications is greater since they proceed one right after another. The block transfer mechanism in the GP1000 which is utilized in the LC scheme holds a message path open for as long as it is needed to transfer the data. Therefore, more collisions are likely to occur in this algorithm due to the increased number of messages required, resulting in high network contention.

5.2.1.4. Load Imbalance (1.5% - 6.9%)

The goal of better load balancing was achieved in this algorithm, using a smaller granularity ratio than the rectangular region approach. The percentage overhead for load imbalance varies from 1.5% for the stegosaurus and mountain images to 6.9% for the Laser image. This algorithm achieves better load balancing than the previous algorithm, with minimal expense required to build the hierarchical tree data structure. It therefore overcomes the limitation noticed in Whelan's and Roble's algorithms, which also used a data adaptive scheme. More details on the overhead time required for the tree construction are given in chapter 6.

5.2.1.5. Code Modification (2.5% - 3.3%)

The overhead due to code modification is much smaller than in the rectangular region approach. This overhead ranges from 2.5% for the mountain image to 3.3% for the Laser image. The reason for the reduction is that there are fewer total tasks and each task area is larger, reducing the overall coherence loss.

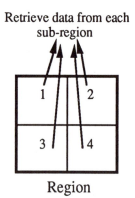

Figure 5.21: Block transfer of data from sub-regions for top-down decomposition

Looking back at figure 5.21, it can be seen that it is likely that a number of polygons cross over several sub-regions but are singularly contained within the main region to be rendered. Unfortunately, short of a direct comparison of all polygons there is no way to detect if a given sub-region is sending the same polygon as another sub-region, due to the usage of the LC memory referencing scheme. If a polygon is sent from two or more different sub-regions as a result of its overlapping these regions, that polygon is rendered more than once. This is a direct function of the duplication factor for the given mesh size. The overhead of this occurrence is difficult to determine since not all polygons which are duplicated are rendered more than once, only those that are duplicated across sub-regions and are part of the same higher region. This duplication of rendering is included in the code modification overhead given previously.

5.2.1.6. Explanation of Results

The goal of the data adaptive top-down scheme is to maintain good load balancing. The implementation here achieves this goal, but due to the method of data transfer required by the LC scheme, additional contention is introduced. There is also the additional cost of constructing the tree data structure, but this cost is offset by the reduction in the number of regions resulting in reduced code modification overhead. The times for the tree building are not included here since this chapter deals with a comparison of the algorithms' tiling section, but they are given in the next chapter. The chart in figure 5.22 shows the overhead comparison for the various images.

It can be seen that all of the overhead factors have been reduced compared to the previous approaches, with the exception of network contention. This algorithm requires a dense mesh to be created for determination of the regions. As P is increased, the mesh will need to be even denser, and this may result in even higher network contention overhead and duplication of polygons. As a result, this algorithm may not exhibit good scalability for very dense meshes.

It might be possible to create the mesh in some other manner which does not result in as much overhead, but other methods were not explored here. For example, if one were to try to determine the clusters from the top down, a pseudo-parallel method could be used whereby tasks are spawned off according to the level of the tree traversed. A large amount of synchronization would be necessary to implement this technique, and the result might involve more overhead than in the current implementation. One of the problems with the algorithms discussed thus far is that they rely on a good choice for the granularity ratio.

Unfortunately, empirical testing must be employed to determine what the best value is for a given situation. In fact, it is possible that the value might need to be changed when the number of processors is increased significantly beyond 96. The next section covers an algorithm that does not rely on a pre-determined granularity ratio, but instead achieves load balancing by dynamically partitioning existing tasks into smaller ones when a processor needs work.

5.3. Task Adaptive Partitioning Scheme

The task adaptive methodology relies on an algorithm's capability to dynamically partition tasks as the program is running. If tasks cannot be adaptively partitioned, then that algorithm is not well suited for dynamic task splitting. Fortunately, the serial scan line Z-buffer algorithm upon which these parallel algorithms are based consists of independent regions, and there is no required order of execution between these regions. The task adaptive algorithm consists of the following steps:

1. When a processor needs work (call this processor P_s), it searches among the other processors for the one which contains

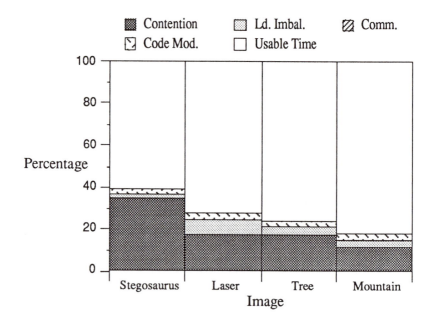

Figure 5.22: Degradation factors for top-down decomposition ($P = 96$)

the most amount of work left to do (call this processor P_{max}).

2. The P_s processor then sets a lock preventing any other processor from splitting P_{max}.

3. P_s partitions P_{max}'s work into two segments; the first segment goes to P_{max} and the second segment goes to P_s.

4. P_s then copies the data necessary for it to work on the second segment.

5. P_s unsets the lock and starts doing its work.

This task adaptive scheme could be tacked onto any of the previous algorithms, so that additional load balancing would be ensured toward the end of the computation. For the implementation here, the rectangular region decomposition scheme was chosen as a basis parallel algorithm since it is fairly simple to work with in developing the heuristic for step 1. A description of this parallel algorithm is given next.

Instead of attempting to choose an optimal granularity ratio, the number of areas is initially set equal to the number of processors ($R = 1$). When a processor has finished computing its area, it executes steps 1 through 5 above. In order to do this, it was necessary to come up with a method for determining the amount of work a given processor has left to do. Since all of the areas are the same size, the number of scan lines left to render in a particular area is used as an indication of how much work there is left on a given processor. This proceeds as follows.

During the tiling portion of the computation, each processor updates a shared variable corresponding to the number of scan lines it has left to compute. P_s quickly runs through these variables checking for the processor that has the maximum number of scan lines left. Once it finds the processor with the most scan lines left (P_{max}), P_s proceeds to split P_{max} as is shown in figure 5.23. Color plate 4 shows an illustration of this process after completion. P_{max} is not interrupted during this time.

The splitting mechanism prevents a race condition from occuring if several processors attempt to split the same region simultaneously or, alternatively, P_{max} attempts to work on a portion of its region which is to be split. The first instance is solved by using a test and lock methodology in which a splitting processor checks to see if P_{max} is currently being split and if so, this splitting processor finds another processor to split. The second case is solved by updating a shared variable which P_{max} checks to determine the last scan line for it to calculate. Neither case requires P_{max} to be interrupted from its work, thus avoiding any synchronization delay.

A threshold must be chosen which limits partitioning of tasks when the cost of the actual partition exceeds the cost of running the task serially. Through empirical testing, it was determined that partitioning a task with only two scan lines left does in fact yield good performance, so this was the threshold limit set. A task which contains no polygons is not allowed to be split since the only work involved is sending the scan lines to the virtual frame buffer.

Since P_s splits P_{max} into two tasks, it makes sense for P_{max} to continue working on the upper task while P_s takes the lower one. This allows coherence to be maintained in P_{max}'s region without any additional overhead. The performance for the task adaptive scheme is given in figure 5.24. The speedup for this scheme is shown in figure 5.25. Although a bit of extra coding is required to handle the splitting operation and data retrieval processes, the algorithm is fairly straightforward to implement.

During the splitting process, it is necessary for the P_s processor to obtain data from the P_{max} processor. Instead of determining exactly which data is relevant to the region that P_s will work on and retrieving only this data, it is simpler for P_s to retrieve all of the data from P_{max} and discard the portion that is not relevant to this new region. This requires a bit of extra communication, but the overhead is minimal compared to any method where either P_s or P_{max} would try to determine the exact relevant data. This is due to the fact that extra synchronization would be required in determining the exact dataset, whereas the "copy and discard" method requires no synchronization at all.

We now analyze the task adaptive scheme with regard to the various overhead factors. One of the problems in determining these

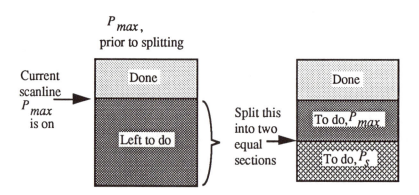

Figure 5.23: Dynamic splitting of regions for task adaptive scheme

factors is the measurement of the total number of tasks. A new task occurs when a processor tries to split another region. The task time includes the time to split a processor's work plus the rendering time. Since the number of tasks varies somewhat depending on the run, it was determined based on an average of five runs. This number varied by less than 1%, so the average is a fairly good indication of what might be considered the actual number of tasks.

5.3.1. Scheduling (0.00006% - 0.00023%)

The number of areas in this scheme is not known ahead of time since the tasks adapt to the work available. Once all of the regions are started, parallel scheduling ceases since the task adaptation is then run on each processor locally. Therefore, the total scheduling time is just T_{crit} * 96 or 2.3 msec. This represents an overhead ranging from 0.00006% for the mountain image to 0.00023% for the stegosaurus image.

5.3.2. Synchronization (0.16% - 2.3%)

It is necessary to determine the amount of time wasted by spinning in a lock, in addition to the extra work needed to determine which processor to split. These two factors constitute the synchronization overhead which was given in equation 4.9. The value for this overhead varies from 0.16% for the tree image to 2.3% for the Laser image. While the time wasted in synchronizing may not be particularly small in some cases, it is necessary in order to facilitate the dynamic partitioning scheme of the task adaptive algorithm.

5.3.3. Communication Overhead (0.11% - 4.2%)

The communication overhead in this algorithm is measured the same as the previous algorithms. The overhead varies from 0.11% for the stegosaurus image to 4.2% for the Laser image. The number of bytes communicated in this algorithm is much higher here than in the other approaches, which accounts for the higher overhead percentage. The reason for this is given next.

At the time a task is split, the splitting processor (P_s) retrieves *all* of the data relevant to the splittee (P_{max}). The data which is unnecessary for the portion of the task which P_s is to work on is then discarded. At the end of the computation, a large amount of splitting occurs due to dynamic load balancing.

Task Adaptive Algorithm (LC Scheme) Performance

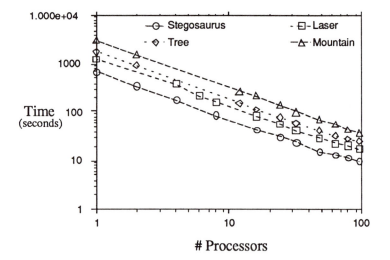

Figure 5.24: Tiling time for task adaptive scheme

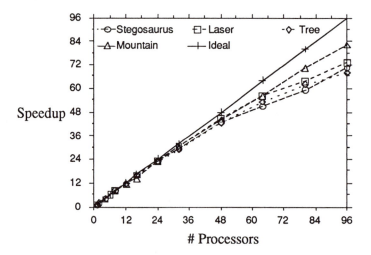

Figure 5.25: Speedup of task adaptive scheme

The areas to be split at this point in the computation are small, but the amount of data to be transferred is large since it is derived from the initial decomposition area. This creates communication of unnecessary data, which is then discarded. Reducing this communication requires extra synchronization, but preliminary studies indicated that performance degraded even worse than if it was not done. In the case of the Laser image, most of the initial areas assigned as work involve background color. These processors finish quickly and then start splitting other processors' work. Since the few processors which are split contain the bulk of the data, a lot of communication occurs. A solution which relieves the extra data transfer in this situation would reduce the communication and contention overheads if it were possible to implement it without significantly increasing the synchronization costs.

5.3.4. Network Contention (5.5% - 11.7%)

The overhead percentage for network contention ranges from 5.5% for the mountain image to 11.7% for the stegosaurus image. Even with the extra communication, the contention measured in this algorithm is only slightly higher than in the rectangular region (LC) scheme.

5.3.5. Load Imbalance (9.2% - 22.5%)

This algorithm tries to minimize load imbalance by using heuristics to dynamically split tasks during parallel execution. The limit of the task size which can be split is set to two scan lines. The load imbalance overhead percentages vary from 9.2% for the mountain image to 22.5% for the tree image. If the only tasks that are left are single scan line tasks, processors which are idle will not be able to find a task to work on. Since the granularity of tasks which cannot be split (a single scan line within an area) is fairly large, the idle time for a processor with no work left can be high, resulting in additional load imbalance. Of course single scan line tasks could be split into two parts as well, but this feature has not been implemented at this point. Further research is needed to see if these tasks can be split, or if some other solution is possible to reduce the excess idle time.

5.3.6. Code Modification (0.4% - 1.5%)

The code modification overhead is measured the same as in the other algorithms. The overhead percentages are fairly small and range in value from 0.4% for the stegosaurus image to 1.5% for the Laser image. These figures are expected since the number of tasks is the smallest of all the algorithms. Consequently, most of the tasks consist of large areas where coherence is maintained. In addition, even when a task is split, the split processor is not interrupted and coherence is not lost for its task.

5.3.7. Explanation of Results

The task adaptive method is an attempt to directly load balance the system by dynamically extracting work when a given processor would otherwise be idle. The solution allows a granularity ratio of $R = 1$ for the initial decomposition. A graph showing the primary overhead contributors is given in figure 5.26.

Unfortunately, the load balancing of this scheme was not as good as was anticipated. Since load balancing is due to the total idle time at the end of the computation, this suggests that processors have quit looking for work too early. The threshold for splitting work imposed here is that a single scan line task cannot be split. Perhaps a scheme could be worked out to allow horizontal splitting, but this would be

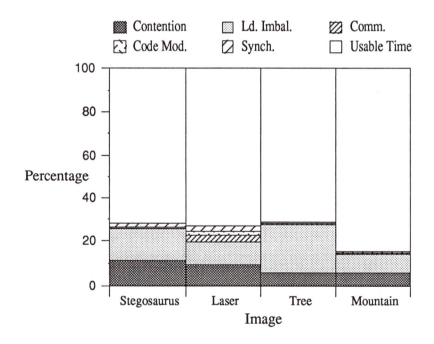

Figure 5.26: Degradation factors for task adaptive algorithm ($P = 96$)

difficult to implement and the synchronization involved may outweigh the benefit of splitting.

Synchronization is an additional overhead in this algorithm, but it was not a significant factor in performance degradation. The communication cost in this algorithm is somewhat larger than the other LC schemes, due to the dynamic partitioning of this dataset. The code modification here is the smallest of all the algorithms since the number of areas generated is initially equal to P. In addition, coherence is maintained in the upper portion of a split area reducing the parallel execution overhead. Network contention seems to be only slightly worse than in the rectangular region (LC) scheme. Toward the end of the computation when dynamic load balancing is taking place, there is a flurry of communication, and this causes network contention to increase at this point. The burst of communication is due to the dynamic splitting of small tasks at the end of the computation. Reducing this last amount of communication is rather difficult in the LC scheme: the reason is described next.

In the task adaptive algorithm, the splitting processor copies all of the data necessary for the entire original size area and then deletes the excess data locally. Ideally, it would be desirable to only copy the data which is needed for the scan lines for which this processor is responsible. The time required to do this would be prohibitive since there are only two ways: 1) the splitting processor remotely determines which polygons are relevant or 2) the processor being split must be synchronized to stop what it is doing and then determine which polygons are relevant for the splitting processor. The first method would require more communication than in the current implementation. The second method requires extra synchronization, plus P_{max} would have to construct a new data structure, and this takes time away from its primary work. Thus, when using the LC scheme, it only makes sense to copy all of the data for the area. In the next chapter, the performance of the task adaptive scheme is analyzed using both the UD and LC memory referencing schemes for the entire program, to see if any difference is noted.

In an attempt to explore other load balancing strategies, different heuristics were tried in order to estimate the maximally loaded processor. For instance, instead of just using the number of scan lines left as the heuristic, the total number of polygons per scan line for all the scan lines left was used. The idea was to evaluate the work in terms of polygons since the lower half of a region to be split could possibly contain no polygons. This method required the splitting processor to retrieve from shared memory an additional value which corresponded to the heuristic. It was also necessary to update this heuristic from scan line to scan line, whereas the previous heuristic required just a simple subtraction operation. As a result, the benefit of this new heuristic was outweighed by its cost, and it proved to have worse performance than the simple one.

Finally, as was mentioned previously, it may be worthwhile to try breaking scan lines into half scan lines to allow a splitting processor to split single scan lines. This would require extra synchronization, but it is possible that the load imbalance would be reduced if the overhead to do this is small. This was not implemented in the test program, and could be done as part of future research.

This algorithm does exhibit good scalability since the algorithm adapts to the scene and divides the tasks accordingly. Its principal advantage is that the number of tasks does not need to be chosen initially, making the granularity ratio analysis unnecessary. In addition, in the next chapter it is shown that the overhead in the front end for this scheme is less than in the other algorithms due to the reduction in the total tasks required in the initial decomposition.

5.4. Conclusions

In this chapter, the maximum potential performance for each of the implemented algorithms is evaluated. This is done by analyzing the tiling portion of the programs. A summary of the results obtained with regard to the influence of the various overhead factors is presented next.

The scheduling overhead is minimal for all of the algorithms discussed here. Since the execution time for the simplest task (background color) is greater than the critical time needed for scheduling, this overhead is not a factor in performance degradation in any of the algorithms.

Synchronization is an important consideration in the task adaptive algorithm due to the dynamic task partitioning. The overhead of synchronization does not degrade the performance significantly, as it turns out, so it is not considered to be a major degradation factor.

The issues of latency, communication, and network contention are all intertwined since they are related to passing data through the interconnection network. Memory latency is relevant to the scan line algorithm and the rectangular region algorithm since those algorithms are implemented using the UD memory referencing scheme. The latency is somewhat smaller for the latter method, due to the reduction in the number of remote memory requests as a result of better exploitation of coherence. Communication comes into play for the LC schemes and results in more efficient use of the interconnection network, with the benefit being a reduction in contention. Graphs which show the total amount of performance degradation for each image are included here so that all of the algorithms may be compared side by side. These are shown in figures 5.27 through 5.30 at the end of the chapter. The graphs are shown in such a way that the total of each column is the total processor-time space. This is the same as the parallel execution time T_p multiplied by the number of processors P (in this case, $P = 96$). Therefore, the column with the least height is the best performing algorithm for that particular image. Based on the data shown in these graphs, one can see that the rectangular region (LC) algorithm results in the lowest overheads, and consequently the best performance in the tiling section.

Hot spot contention is not a factor in any of these algorithms. This is because the large data structures are distributed across the memory modules. Copying of small data structures to local memory is also employed if these structures are referenced frequently. Although there may be frequent references to common data structures, this method of scattered storage ensures that performance is not degraded since no hot spots exist in any of the programs.

Load balancing is a primary goal of any parallel implementation. The only algorithm in which the load imbalance is significantly reduced is the data adaptive algorithm. The task adaptive algorithm exhibits the worst load balancing of all the algorithms. The probable reason for this is the lack of splitting at the scan line level (that is, below the threshold). Surprisingly, the scan line algorithm does not exhibit much worse load balancing than the others. This changes as the number of processors is increased since the number of tasks available for each processor is reduced.

The primary overhead due to code modification is the loss of coherence. The parallel scan line algorithm exhibits total loss of vertical scan line coherence. The number of regions created in the two rectangular region schemes introduces some loss of coherence in both the horizontal and vertical directions. Since the top-down and task adaptive algorithms require fewer regions than any of the other approaches, the code modification overhead for these methods is small.

Scalability is one of the most important characteristics of a parallel algorithm. In evaluating these implementations, it seems evident that the parallel scan line algorithm does not exhibit particularly good scalability. In table 5.2, each of the implemented algorithms is compared for each image, using 96 processors. The times listed are an average of 3 runs, although the difference between each run was less than 1%.

From the table we can see that the data non-adaptive rectangular region (LC) scheme provides the best results in most cases. The comparison is only for the tiling section of the program and does not include the overheads inherent in each of the LC algorithms. Also, the overhead of building the tree data structure necessary for the the top-down data adaptive algorithm is not included. It is important to not make any judgments as to the usefulness of any of these algorithms at this point since there are numerous other factors that must be examined to determine how well they will perform in the general case. The analysis here is purely with respect to the performance of the tiling section of the algorithms since this section of the program is where the most parallelism can be exploited.

Table 5.2: Comparative times in seconds of tiling for all algorithms on 96 processors

	UD Scheme		LC Scheme		
Images	Scan line	Rect. Region (UD)	Rect. Region (LC)	Top-Down Adaptive	Task Adaptive
Stegosaurus	12.66	13.38	10.16	12.93	9.94
Laser	21.29	19.94	17.06	18.72	18.33
Tree	24.88	25.70	22.72	23.66	26.41
Mountain	59.85	44.33	38.35	40.31	39.98

The setup operations prior to the tiling section vary depending on the algorithm used for task decomposition. If these costs are high for a particular method, the overall performance is affected. These costs are included in the analysis in the next chapter to give a better overall view of the performance of the implementations. The different shared memory referencing strategies are investigated and analyzed in the next chapter as well.

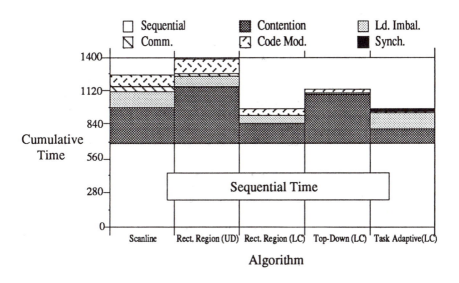

Figure 5.27: Comparison of overheads for algorithms, stegosaurus image

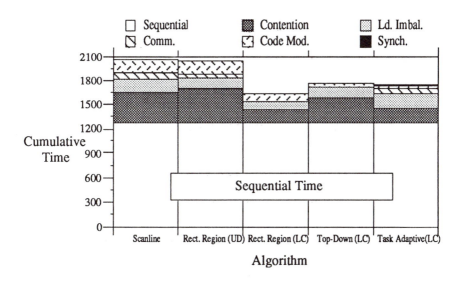

Figure 5.28: Comparison of overheads for algorithms, Laser image

Overhead Comparison, All Algorithms

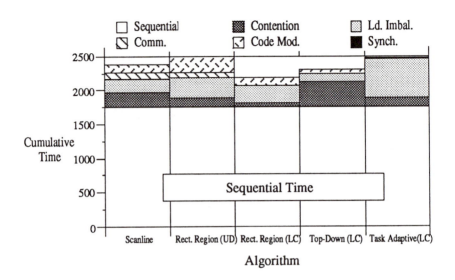

Figure 5.29: Comparison of overheads for algorithms, tree image

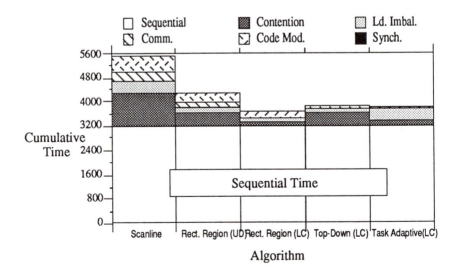

Figure 5.30: Comparison of overheads for algorithms, mountain image

6

Characterization of Other Parameters on Performance

In this chapter, a number of parameters are investigated which differ from those discussed thus far. The purpose here is to produce a comprehensive study of the shared memory referencing strategies and further evaluate the performance of the various algorithms under a variety of conditions. Several different shared memory storage and referencing methods are analyzed in the first section. The implementations of the Uniformly Distributed and Locally Cached schemes are described in detail in this section. A framework is presented which allows a straightforward comparison of these schemes using the task partitioning implementations discussed in the previous chapter. In the second section, the effect of machine parameters such as the operating system and architectural characteristics are evaluated in regard to algorithm performance. In the third section, a number of additional characteristics such as image and object complexity are varied to see how overall algorithmic performance is affected. The comparisons in this chapter are intended to provide a broader base for determining the relative merits of each of the parallel approaches which have been implemented.

6.1. Shared Memory Storage and Referencing

The idea of partitioning image space segments for use in a parallel graphics rendering algorithm can be extended to memory referencing as well. The scene data used in the graphics rendering algorithms is read in from disk and then processed in the front end. The polygons are then transformed from three-dimensional space to image space and become read-only data thereafter. As such, the read-only data can be partitioned in numerous ways for referencing during the tiling portion of the program. Three alternative data storage and access schemes for use in a parallel graphics display algorithm are presented in the subsections which follow. A brief description of these schemes is given next.

If enough memory is available, all of the data could be copied to each processor's local memory; then no remote memory access is necessary after the copying phase is completed. This storage and access scheme is analyzed in the first subsection below. The second scheme involves scattering the data among the memory modules in the system and referencing it remotely. In the third technique, the data is scattered initially as in the second scheme, but then a reorganization is required to allow the data to be copied to the local processor's memory as it is needed. This last method allows local referencing after the copy is completed and is described in the third subsection. The second and third methods are the same as the UD and LC memory referencing strategies discussed previously. Here, their theoretical performance is analyzed, and a full description of the implementation details is presented.

A dataset which would contain 100,000 points and 100,000 polygons is used for theoretical analysis. The front end process removes a number of backfacing polygons, conservatively eliminating 1/3 of the original data (this assumes a given polygon is not both front and backfacing). Below, the amount of memory required for this dataset is given after transformations and backface rejection have been applied. The assumption in this case is that a mesh of size 48 x 48 has been placed over the image. This corresponds to the number of regions generated with a granularity ratio of $R = 24$ on 96 processors using the rectangular region task partitioning scheme.

When applying a mesh over the image, a polygon (or polygon pointer) needs to be duplicated for each region that a given polygon crosses over. This duplication is based on both the size of the polygons and the granularity of the mesh. The mountain image contains approximately 83,000 polygons after backfaces are removed. As an example of the duplication, figure A.12 in the appendix shows that for this image, 130,000 polygons are created after duplication using a 48 x 48 mesh which is an increase of 57%. Using the 100,000 polygon test situation and this same percentage increase as an example, we can expect to lose 33,333 polygons to backface rejection and then gain 57% more polygons from duplication, resulting in a final total of 105,000 polygons. We assume that this results in 105,000 points as well, although this latter value is typically smaller.

The analyses given next take into account the additional time required to access data beyond a normal local memory access. This includes any setup time specific to each scheme in addition to any latency incurred.

6.1.1. Copy Data to all Processors

This method involves copying all the data to all of the processors in the system. No remote referencing is required after the data is copied, so no communication overhead is incurred during the tiling portion of the program. To ascertain the cost of copying the data to all processors, let us estimate the time to copy 105,000 points and 105,000 polygons to 96 processors. This copying can be accomplished in parallel by creating a binary tree of processes in which the data is copied throughout the network from processors that contain data to neighboring ones that do not. This copying process is repeated until all processors contain data. The number of times this is repeated is the height of the tree, namely ceil($\log_2$(96)) or 7. Each data point contains 3 floating point values consuming 12 bytes, and it is assumed that each polygon is a quadrilateral. Using the storage data format described previously in section 4.1.1, a single polygon takes up 10 bytes.

The memory required for all the data is then 105,000 * (12 + 10) or 2.31 million bytes. Equation 6.1 shows the communication cost with block transfers of 256 bytes, each using the binary tree copying technique.

$$T_{comm} = \#levels \; * \; \#transfers \; * \; (T_{setup} + 256 \; {}^*T_{bt}) \qquad (6.1)$$

T_{setup} is 8 μsec and T_{bt} is 0.25 μsec/byte for block transfers on the Butterfly GP1000. The number of levels is 7, and the number of block transfers is (2.31 million)/256 or 9,023. Plugging these numbers into the equation results in an overhead time of **4.548** seconds. This time does not include the time to copy normals or the polygon information data structure which contains the bounding box of the polygon, a pointer to its location in the polygon list, and other information. If these are required, the time would be more than double, although it is possible to create both data structures locally on each processor instead. The memory required for all of these data structures, in addition to the data structures needed for scan conversion, exceeds the 4 megabyte limit per processor available in the BBN GP1000.

The preceding analysis assumes that no network contention occurs during the copying process. This will not be the case after a few levels of the copying tree have been completed since there are not that many unique switch paths in the Butterfly and some may become blocked. This might be avoided by copying less data simultaneously, but that adds levels to the tree. There is also the issue of copying the normals and other necessary data structures or regenerating these locally. Regenerating the normals adds time to the computation, but not to the copying process. Alternatively, the potential for increased network contention exists if the normals are copied. A more detailed analysis is needed to adequately evaluate this issue, but it is not necessary for the purposes here since conclusions can be drawn without such an analysis.

This copying scheme uses a huge amount of memory so that subsequent references to all data can be local. The amount of data that any processor really needs to perform its tasks is significantly less than the entire input dataset, since each task will likely refer to only a small subset during the tiling operation. Therefore, this scheme makes inefficient use of the network and storage resources. The potential for network contention increases as larger processor configurations are used. The reason is that the number of processors increases linearly, while the number of switch paths increases logarithmically. In addition, more memory is required than is available per processor, so this scheme is not generally usable except for smaller datasets. Even for machines which might have enough memory per processor, it is still evident that this method is inadequate for general use. The next scheme makes better use of the memory in the system.

6.1.2. Global Referencing

The basic idea in global referencing of shared data is to distribute the data and references throughout the system. This avoids hot spot contention since the data is not in a single location, although latency and network contention are introduced during the tiling section. This technique allows the aggregate memory available in the system to be used so that it can be considered as one globally shared memory. The data is stored so there is only one copy in the system, which conserves system memory in addition to the time savings resulting from not copying unnecessary data.

This method is essentially the same as the shared memory storage in bus-based architectures such as the Encore Multimax or Sequent Balance. These computers, known as Uniform Memory Access (UMA) architectures, use such a scheme in all programs since a global view is provided of memory in these architectures. They incorporate a number of different processor boards connected to a bus, on the other side of which is a number of memory boards, as was illustrated in chapter 3, figure 3.2. The term UMA refers to the fact that every processor is the same distance from global memory, resulting in an equally distributed communications overhead. This technique can be emulated in software on the Butterfly, where it will be referred to as the Uniformly Distributed (UD) approach to shared memory referencing. A brief description of this scheme was given in section 4.1.1.2, which presented the design of the front end to all the algorithms. The data is scattered throughout the memory modules as it is read-in and then referenced remotely in the tiling portion of the program. After this scattering of data, each processor contains approximately N/P polygons; that is, the dataset is evenly divided among the memory modules. Since the data is scattered throughout the system uniformly, an average of $1/P$ of the references to shared memory will actually be to data stored locally. Although this percentage is an average, it is likely that the deviation from this average must be large. The worst case situation, where all of the data referenced by a given processor is stored remotely, is actually a more realistic scenario. The reason for this expectation is due to the screen space locality of data. Most of the references for a given task will likely be to a particular processor or group of processors rather than scattered throughout the entire system. An estimate of the remote referencing time overhead in the tiling section using this shared memory referencing strategy is presented here with the assumption that all references to global memory are remote references.

The integration of scattering the data with reading in objects in the front end allows the front end work to be accomplished on each processor without any remote referencing. The time for the front end work does not need to be accounted for in the following analysis since there is no difference among the memory strategies in the way this is performed. The remote referencing time overhead is given in equation 6.2.

$$T_{latency} = \#refs * (T_{rref} - T_{lref})\qquad(6.2)$$

T_{rref} is the remote referencing time which is 7 µsec. T_{lref} is the local referencing time, which is 0.53 µsec. The latency factor is the time difference between these two values. The number of remote references in the tiling section is based on a number of factors. Due to the construction of local edge lists, each point must be referenced 3 times and each polygon once. Since each point contains 3 floats, the number of point references is 3 * 3 * 105,000, or 945,000 point references. The number of polygon references is 105,000 polygons * 5 shorts per polygon, or 525,000. In addition, about 5 references are needed per polygon to obtain the polygon pointer from remote memory, as well as other polygon information adding up to 525,000 more references. There is also one reference for each normal, which results in 3 floats per normal * 105,000, or 315,000 references for normals. The total number of references per processor on 96 processors in parallel is then 1/96 * (945,000 + 525,000 + 525,000 + 315,000) or approximately 24,063 references per processor. The communication time is then: 24,063 * 6.47 µsec or **0.1557** second.

This analysis is *very* simplified since network contention is not taken into consideration. The edge list data is stored locally after it is remotely referenced, so it does not need to be referenced remotely again. A number of remote references to the points list are required in the anti-aliasing portion of the program which are not accounted for in the values derived above. That section of the code could be optimized to allow only one remote reference per point by using temporary storage, but we have not implemented such an optimization. As shown here, the small overhead for this scheme makes it attractive for implementation. Next, the details of implementation are described in regard to this scheme.

Implementation of the UD Scheme

During the front end, as the polygons are read in, it is necessary to determine in which area(s) of the 2D screen mesh a given polygon may belong. A short pseudo-code segment shows how this is done:

```
On each processor:
For all polygons on this processor          O(N/P)
    For all areas in mesh this polygon
    crosses over                            O(c)
        Lock mesh(i,j)
        Load polygon pointer into end of
        area[i][j] linked list
        Unlock mesh(i,j)
```

The time complexity is based on the number of polygons on a given processor after backface rejection (N/P) multiplied by a constant (c). This constant is the number of areas a polygon can cross over, and is related to the size of the polygons and the size of the mesh. The duplication graphs in the appendix in figures A.9 through A.12 indicate the total number of polygons after duplication, based on mesh size. The duplication factor is the number of polygons after duplication divided by the original number of polygons. This factor, which would be the average number of iterations for the inner loop above, goes from approximately 4 for the stegosaurus image to 1.5 for the mountain image, with a mesh size of 48 x 48 (2048 areas). The locks are needed so that only one processor at a time adds a link to the shared link list (area[i][j]). A separate lock exists for each area in the mesh. Figure 6.1 illustrates the storage of polygon pointers in the area mesh.

During the tiling operation, a separate area is assigned to each processor as a single task. The processor then traverses the polygon linked list and constructs local edge lists for use in the tiling operation. The pointers in these links are scattered throughout global memory so a global reference is required for each link, but this is only needed during the initial traversal of the list. These global references are included in the preceding analysis. This implementation of the

Shared Area Mesh

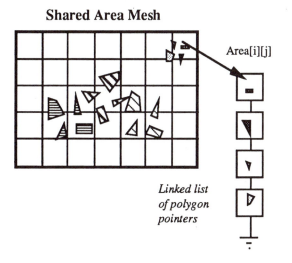

Figure 6.1: Area mesh storage of polygons pointers

Uniformly Distributed (UD) scheme was used in the scan line and rectangular region algorithms described in chapter 5, sections 5.1.1 and 5.1.2.

6.1.3. Software Caching

The last type of referencing scheme is designed to optimize memory access on a Non-Uniform Memory Access or NUMA architecture. The term NUMA refers to the fact that some references to shared data require less time than others since a processor can access shared data stored in its local memory module without retrieving it remotely across the interconnection network. The UMA architectures described previously use a local cache which contains the most recently referenced data, thus allowing (potentially) faster access to the shared data. The UMA architectures use sophisticated cache coherence schemes so that the copy of the data in the cache is the same as what is stored in global memory. NUMA architectures such as the BBN Butterfly typically do not exploit cache coherence (even if they have a cache); the programmer is responsible for maintaining cache coherence. Since cache coherence is not normally available in an NUMA machine, it is not recommended to copy writable shared data to local processor *private* memory. Read-only shared data can be copied to private memory, and the data is then accessible locally, as was the case in the first scheme described previously. In the scheme described here, however, only the data needed for a particular screen area is copied rather than the entire dataset.

Implementation Details for LC Scheme

The method for local referencing we have implemented for NUMA machines is called the Locally Cached (LC) memory referencing scheme. The basic idea is to copy the appropriate data into the local memory of the processor which will use it for tiling a given region. This scheme allows local referencing of data without any latency or possible network contention, except during the copying operation. The data is read in during the front end, as was done in the previous UD scheme. After the front end, each processor contains on its local memory module an average of N/P polygons as before. For this analysis, it is assumed that the 48 x 48 rectangular region partitioning is used as before. The data is arranged into contiguous blocks (arrays) prior to copying in the tiling section. An explanation of why this is done is given after the pseudo-code is presented below. The implementation proceeds as follows:

In Parallel: <u>Complexity</u>
[1st pass]

```
For all polygons on this processor          O(N/P)
    For all areas in mesh this polygon
    crosses over                            O(c)
        Accumulate memory needed for
        each of the following 4 arrays:
        (points,normals,polygon connectivity,polygon info)
```

[2nd pass]

```
For all polygons on this processor          O(N/P)
    For all areas in mesh this polygon
    crosses over                            O(c)
        Allocate memory for each of 4 arrays
        for area[i][j] if not done yet
        Add polygon and point data to
        the 4 arrays listed above
Free up original scattered data.
```

This code is executed prior to the tiling section of the program and was not included in the measurements in chapter 5. The first pass is necessary to determine how much memory to allocate for a particular region, and the second pass actually allocates the memory on the local processor and copies the data into it. A barrier synchronization is necessary between the passes so that the data is updated properly for all regions. All of the work in these phases is done using local memory, so no remote referencing occurs here. The inner loops in the first and second passes are of the same time complexity as the inner loop described in the previous section. Figure 6.2 illustrates the storage of the arrays in each local processor's memory.

Local Area Mesh

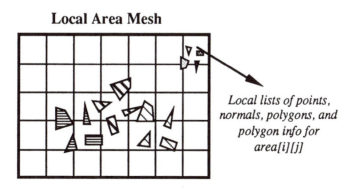

Local lists of points, normals, polygons, and polygon info for area[i][j]

Figure 6.2: Locally cached memory storage mechanism

The LC method is more than just a "block copy then local reference" scheme. It consists of a complicated set of instructions which involve constructing data structures for later block transfer. The principal advantage of this scheme in a non-blocking network such as in the Butterfly is as follows. The setup cost is incurred only once for a block of data, and thereafter the message proceeds at the full bandwidth of the interconnection network. This is faster than individually copying each remote value to local memory since the setup time for that method would be incurred for each single reference. The disadvantage to this block copy method is that the data must be arranged into a contiguous array. If a blocking interconnection network were to be used, the data could then be transferred byte by byte instead. The LC scheme consists of a method of organizing data primarily for later local referencing while using minimal memory usage. The data structures and setup routines necessary to achieve this set it apart from a pure software caching scheme.

The pseudo-code presented for this scheme sets up the blocks for copying, but the copying phase is actually executed during the tiling portion of the program. If a completely uniform distribution of the data occurs, then each processor would contain exactly $1/P$ of the data for a particular area. In general, this is not the case, as was stated before based on the locality of screen space data. For this analysis, it is assumed that the data is distributed in such a way to encounter a worst case scenario (i.e., all the data needed for each region is stored remotely). For a particular task, it is necessary to use P separate block transfer groups to retrieve the data. This is shown in figure 6.3 on the next page.

To simplify matters, each processor is assumed to execute exactly R tasks so that the total number of block transfer groups is $(4 * R * P)$. Four refers to the fact that it is necessary to retrieve the points, normals, polygon connectivity, and polygon info arrays separately. Each block transfer retrieves on average $1/(R * P)$ of the total amount of data.

Based on the analysis at the beginning of this section, the total amount of data after backface rejection and duplication is 105,000 polygons, so the amount of data per area of the 48 x 48 mesh is approximately 46 polygons. Recall that for a block transfer, T_{setup} is 8 μsec and T_{bt} is 0.25 μsec/byte. If the data is evenly scattered as was stated above, each polygon (in the worst case) is on a separate processor, requiring 46 separate groups of 4 block transfers each.

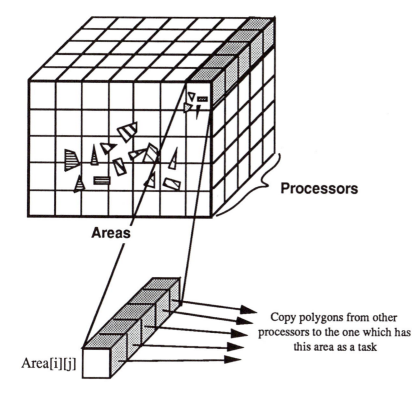

Processors

Areas

Area[i][j]

Copy polygons from other
processors to the one which has
this area as a task

Figure 6.3: Block transfer of data

The data is scattered among the 46 processors which contain polygons for a given area, so the total time to retrieve data for one region is 46 * 38.5 μsec or 1.77 msec. Since each processor works on an average of 24 regions, the total time for a processor to retrieve all the data it needs to work on its regions during the tiling section is 24 * 1.77 msec or **0.0425** second. Again, it is assumed that no network contention exists for this analysis. This time is executed in parallel so 0.0425 second is the parallel communication time. The time for block transfer for a single polygon is then:

Block	Time
1. 10 bytes/polygon	7.5 μsec
2. 20 bytes for polygon info	15.0 μsec
3. 12 bytes/point • 4 points/polygon	8.0 μsec
4. 12 bytes/normal • 4 normals/polygon	8.0 μsec
Total	38.5 μsec

This time is significantly better than any of the times listed above for the previous methods of memory storage. The second pass is necessary to set up the arrays for block transferring, but this has not been taken into account in the preceding analysis. Since this time is extra, it needs to be accounted for as well. In the next paragraph, the second pass algorithm is described, and its time complexity is analyzed.

In the second pass, new arrays are constructed which correspond to the data that is relevant to each area of the 2D mesh in the local processor. In constructing these new arrays, it is desirable to not create any unnecessary new data points. In order to do this, a backwards reference list is used to determine which points have been stored in this area thus far. In order to keep the amount of memory within limits for this backwards reference list, a fairly sophisticated data structure is used. This data structure is an array which corresponds to the points list, but contains links which indicate when any point that has been previously stored in this area is part of a new polygon. The backwards reference list data structure is shown in figure 6.4.

The diagram shows that the backwards reference list corresponds to each point in the original object. The small array to the right is used to indicate the areas each point is referenced in (the polygons which contain it can be in more than one area) and the value of the point's index for the new points list in each of these areas. The new points list allows us to sequentially go through the polygon list in the front end. This data structure uses less memory than a separate backwards list array for each area since that type of list would be relatively sparse. The list requires some time to manage, and this time is considered as part of the analysis.

The backwards reference list is also required for the first pass, but in that case the reason is to determine how much memory to allocate for the contiguous arrays. The top loop given in the pseudo-code is of time complexity $O(N/P)$ which in the case given here corresponds to approximately 1094 polygons. The inner loop would be approximately of time complexity (constant = 2) for a theoretical 100,000 polygon dataset based on the analysis of the mountain image, but we will use the value (constant = 4) for a possible worst case scenario. The management of the backwards reference list requires us to run through each point in the polygon, so there really is a third inner loop that would be of time complexity (constant = 4), assuming quadrilateral polygons. The only difference between the first pass and the second pass is the time required to allocate memory for the areas not already allocated and to store the data in the new arrays while updating the count for these lists. The GP1000 contains 2.5 MIPS MC68020 processors, and based on the amount of work in the inner loop of the second pass, we estimate the time to complete this operation to be 20 μsec per iteration. This results in a time for the second pass of 1094 * 4 * 4 * 20 μsec or **0.35** second. This analysis is simplified, but the purpose is to show the additional overhead incurred by the LC scheme. The first pass time is not measured since

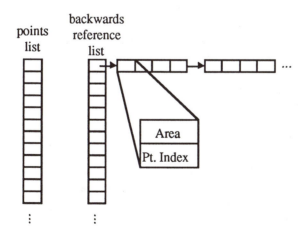

Figure 6.4: Backwards reference list data structure

it takes approximately the same amount of time as its counterpart loop in the UD scheme. The total time for this scheme is then 0.35 seconds for the second pass plus the time of 0.0425 second for communication, resulting in a sum total of **0.3925** second.

There have been several other graphics algorithms which incorporate the idea of local caching in a distributed memory environment. Green and Paddon [Gree89] as well as Badouel, *et al.* [Bado90] have both implemented a software caching mechanism in a distributed memory environment. Both algorithms use ray tracing for hidden surface elimination and rely on the concept of ray coherence for minimizing remote references. Ray coherence is defined to be the property in which rays in adjacent pixels are likely to intersect the same objects. Once these objects are brought into the local memory of a processor by the cache mechanism, the rays sent out by this processor will intersect these same objects in local memory. Based on this fact, Badouel was able to achieve a 95% or better hit ratio into the caches. An area screen space distribution of the pixels to processors is used for task decomposition, similar to the approaches given here.

These algorithms were designed to allow one to distribute a large graphical database on a message passing multiprocessor such as the Intel iPSC, which provides no support for shared memory referencing. The caching employed in Green's algorithm involves statically partitioning local memory for caching purposes, while Badouel's method uses a more dynamic approach without any preprocessing. Badouel's algorithm allows virtual memory to be distributed by taking advantage of the aggregate memory in the system, whereas Green's approach requires the host to maintain virtual memory. In Badouel's algorithm, the object database is statically divided up into pages and scattered throughout the system in a way similar to the scattering of data used in the LC scheme described previously. If a page is not resident in the local processor's memory or cache, the page is retrieved from the processor memory module where it is resident and put into the local processor's cache using a least recently used (LRU) cache replacement policy. Badouel has shown significant speedup on the Intel iPSC with this caching scheme built into a multiprocessor ray tracing algorithm. Several faults exist with this scheme if it is to be applied to a conventional scan line algorithm such as those outlined in the previous chapter.

The first issue is the amount of memory available in each processor. A ray tracing algorithm might use a hierarchical tree structure such as an octree to speed up calculating ray-object intersections, and this tree must be stored in all processor memories.

No other additional memory is required during the execution of the program. In a scan line algorithm, edge lists, anti-aliasing data structures, and interpolation parameter arrays must be built which all take up a significant amount of local memory. More local memory is necessary in a scan line algorithm than is needed for ray tracing, so less would be available for the cache. The reduction in cache size would result in a lower hit ratio, giving lower performance. In a ray tracing algorithm, it is impossible to know a priori which polygons might be needed in local memory since a ray can be spawned to any direction in three-dimensional space. It therefore makes sense to bring in the data as needed using a LRU replacement policy. In the algorithms presented in the previous chapter, the exact polygons that are needed for rendering are known ahead of time, so only those should be brought into the local memory module. Furthermore, since those polygons are only used for a single task, the original (remotely stored) polygons can be deleted. This provides additional free space, allowing more room for local data structures.

The second issue is the amount of communication and potential contention problems in the caching mechanism. The amount of memory brought in using the LC scheme is exactly what is needed, so no unnecessary message traffic is required. Badouel's caching scheme copies pages one at a time, and it possible that only one item of an entire page is required. The results of speedup in his ray tracing algorithm are based on images which take minutes to render on 64 processors and would typically take hours to render on a single processor. This is due to the fact that ray tracing is a slower, less efficient rendering algorithm than the image space methods described in this document. The ratio of computation time to message traffic time is so high in ray tracing that any possible bottlenecks in message passing are masked due to the high computation time. The higher efficiency of the scan line algorithm reduces computation time, so these bottlenecks are more likely to degrade overall performance than in a less efficient algorithm. This is shown by the reduction in network contention determined for the larger datasets using the LC algorithms in the previous chapter. Badouel's approach requires more communication than the LC scheme given here since pages are brought into memory as needed. Therefore, his approach is likely to result in greater contention when compared to the LC scheme. While a multiprocessor can sufficiently speed up a costly algorithm such as ray tracing, the benefits of using that type of method are generally not needed in most applications. The real need by most scientists and other users is to be able to display extremely complex datasets in a reasonable amount of time. Therefore, if reflections are needed, one should use a ray tracer. If high quality scenes need to be generated quickly without reflections, an image space algorithm such as those illustrated here is more appropriate.

In the next section, the results of the UD and LC schemes are compared, including the overheads required in the front end and the second pass, to see how these affect the overall performance of each of the algorithms.

6.1.4. Results

The total time for remote referencing of the LC scheme is **0.3925** versus the time of **0.1557** second in the UD scheme based on the theoretical analysis used here. On the surface it would seem that the UD scheme is the better alternative even with its remote reference strategy. However, one important factor missing from this analysis is network contention. From the data given in chapter 5, contention contributed significantly more to degradation of performance in the UD scheme than in the LC scheme for the rectangular region partitioning scheme. The primary reason is that the LC scheme uses the network in bursts of communication which take a very short amount of time, minimizing the chance of a blocked path. The UD scheme relies on a large number of small messages which can eventually saturate the network.

To illustrate the differences between the two memory referencing strategies, we compare them using the data for the tiling section from chapter 5. The data from running the task adaptive algorithm using the UD scheme has also been included. The UD task adaptive algorithm is not nearly as efficient as the rectangular region UD implementation since each time an area is started, the entire polygon list from the split area must be traversed. These polygons are traversed from shared memory, while in the LC implementation of the task adaptive scheme, local memory is used. Latency causes the algorithm's efficiency to go down as the number of processors is increased.

The graphs for these algorithms for the tiling section time are shown in figures 6.5, 6.6, 6.7, and 6.8. This is the same data that was presented in chapter 5 with the addition of the task adaptive version of the UD scheme, but here all the data is put on the same graph to allow direct comparisons. The comparisons in this case only involve the rectangular region and the task adaptive algorithms since these are the only algorithms which were implemented using both strategies. The data is shown above 48 processors so that the reader may get a clearer idea as to the performance difference, which is mainly evident at high processor configurations. Based on this data, one can see that the LC scheme is consistently better than the UD scheme. While these graphs show that the LC scheme is clearly superior to the UD scheme in the tiling section, it is only fair to look at the total picture. By this we mean that all of the algorithms should be compared by evaluating the parallel execution time plus the setup time from the front end, as shown in the formulas on the page following the graphs. The total front end time will not be included here since disk access is used in that section of the program. Disk access time is affected by other parameters which cannot be controlled unless the machine is put into single user mode. In general, all of the algorithms employ the same disk read-in scheme anyway, so this is not an issue.

The primary differences in the algorithms occur in the following phases:

1. The time to load polygons into the area bucket data structure (or y-bucket list in the case of the parallel scan line algorithm) according to their screen space location.
2. The additional time necessary in the second pass for those algorithms which use the LC scheme.
3. The time to build the hierarchical tree for the data adaptive top-down scheme.
4. The tiling section time.

The table below shows how the comparison times are determined for each algorithm, including the memory referencing scheme and granularity ratio. Using these formulas, a fair comparison of all the algorithms is now possible since the different overheads prior to tiling are included. The primary variation in the setup time is due to the difference in cost for the total number of regions to be started ($R \bullet P$) in the implemented algorithms.

Algorithm (memory scheme)	Phases	Granularity Ratio
Data Non-Adaptive		
Scan line Algorithm (UD):	Phase 1 + Phase 4	(R varies with P)
Rectangular Region (UD):	Phase 1 + Phase 4	($R = 24$)
Rectangular Region (LC):	Phase 1 + Phase 2 + Phase 4	($R = 24$)
Data Adaptive		
Top-Down (LC):	Phase 1 + Phase 2 + Phase 3 + Phase 4	($R = 10$)
Task Adaptive		
Task-Adaptive (UD):	Phase 1 + Phase 4	($R = 1$)
Task-Adaptive (LC):	Phase 1 + Phase 2 + Phase 4	($R = 1$)

UD vs. LC Tiling Section Timing Comparisons

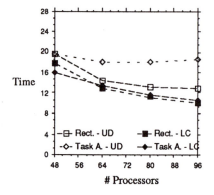

Figure 6.5: UD vs. LC stegosaurus image, tiling section only

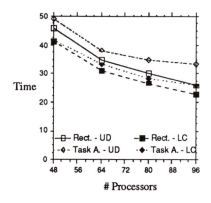

Figure 6.7: UD vs. LC tree image, tiling section only

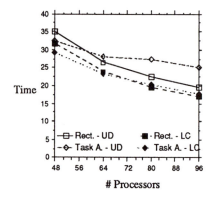

Figure 6.6: UD vs. LC Laser image, tiling section only

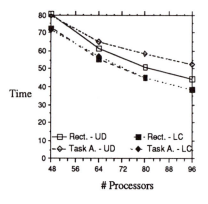

Figure 6.8: UD vs. LC mountain image, tiling section only

The graphs which result from these summations for each algorithm are shown in figures 6.9, 6.10, 6.11, and 6.12. The graphs are shown above 64 processors.

Based on the data shown in these graphs, it can be seen that the task adaptive algorithm utilizing the locally cached (LC) memory referencing scheme is clearly superior for all of the images. This algorithm requires fewer regions at the beginning of the program than any of the other algorithms. The overhead time for loading polygons into the area bucket list, as well as the second pass time, is fairly small as a result. The rectangular region algorithm, which is slightly faster for some images in the tiling section only, requires significantly more setup prior to tiling, degrading overall performance. One might have thought that the second pass section of the LC scheme would require too much setup time to benefit the total algorithmic performance, but this turned out not to be the case. While the second pass does add some time to the LC schemes, the benefits of local referencing in the tiling section far outweigh the cost of the setup operations since they can be done in parallel. This also indicates that network contention is a major factor in the resultant performance of each approach since the disparity in performance is greater than what was indicated in the theoretical analysis from the previous subsection. It seems clear that these results are consistent and valid for the tests done so far, but it is desirable to be able to generalize these statements by evaluating the various algorithms under a variety of other conditions. Some of these conditions are investigated in the next section.

6.2. Machine Parameters

Although the performance of the different algorithms has been analyzed previously, these circumstances represent only one possible machine configuration. There are various hardware and system software changes which may affect overall algorithmic performance, most of which are beyond the programmer's control. These types of parameters are investigated in this section. For instance, the operating system can have a significant impact on performance. In the implementation of the Mach operating system on the GP1000, single jobs are scheduled onto processors based on the current least loaded processor; however, the Uniform System takes over this task within a parallel program. The operating system does intervene to some degree in this machine by handling virtual memory, I/O, and general MACH system operations. Changes in the operating system

All Algorithms Compared including Setup Time

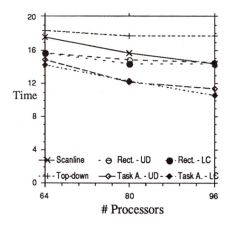

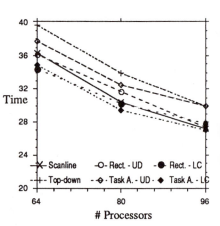

Figure 6.9: All algorithms compared, stegosaurus image, total time

Figure 6.11: All algorithms compared, tree image, total time

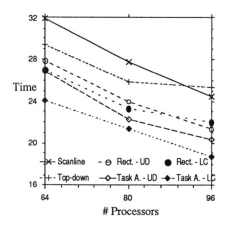

Figure 6.10: All algorithms compared, Laser image, total time

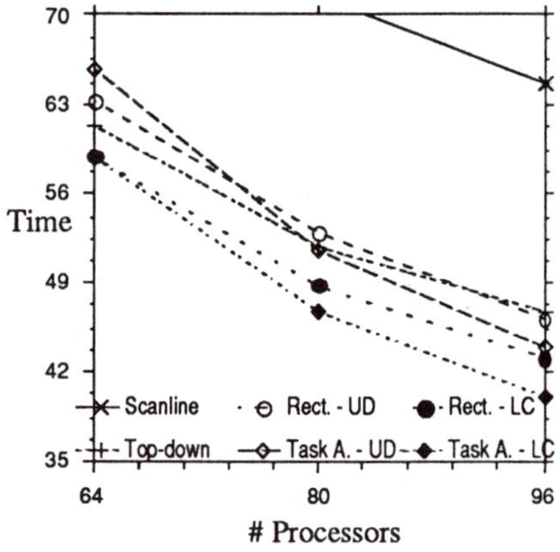

Figure 6.12: All algorithms compared, mountain image, total time

can change program performance; this is described in the first subsection below.

In the second subsection, we investigate the differences in two versions of the Butterfly multiprocessor: the GP1000 and the TC2000. Since the TC2000 is a logical extension of the GP1000 with different physical characteristics, it is interesting to compare the performance of these two machines.

6.2.1. Operating System

Since 1987, BBN has made a number of improvements to the GP1000, but none were so dramatic as the improvement made to the GP1000 version of the Mach operating system in the summer of 1990. The author previously reported preliminary results on this project in [Whit90] early in the summer of 1990, and the limits of the graphs were set to only 32 processors since inconclusive data was obtained above that. The primary reason was the previous version of Mach implemented on the GP1000.[1]

The older version of the GP1000 operating system had the following major problem: when any references occurred to a memory page which was not resident, only one page fault at a time was allowed to be serviced in the entire system. As an example, if processor i had a local page fault and processor j had a local page fault simultaneously, these page faults proceeded only serially even though they had nothing to do with each other. In a graphics algorithm such as the one described here, the amount of memory required is tremendous, and this serial page faulting had an extremely negative impact on performance. BBN rectified this problem and released a new version of the operating system in the summer of 1990; then performance changed dramatically. As an example of the difference in performance, we compare the rectangular region algorithm using the UD scheme in figures A.13, A.14, A.15, and A.16. A comparison of the LC scheme version is shown in figures A.17, A.18, A.19, and A.20. These figures are given in the appendix, but a copy of a representative graph for the mountain data using each of these schemes is shown in figures 6.13 and 6.14 on the next page. All of these graphs are comparisons of the tiling sections only.

As one can see from the graphs, the performance in the old operating system starts to tail off after about 48 processors in the UD scheme. The LC scheme is somewhat better since local rather than

---

[1]Note, the TC2000 has had the new version of the operating system since its delivery in the beginning of 1990.

global data referencing is taking place, although performance tails off here as well. Unfortunately, the amount of testing done using the old operating system was limited, so additional results could not be obtained. It is clear from these results, though, that the operating system in a shared memory multiprocessor has significant impact on the overall performance. We feel confident that the latest version of the GP1000 operating system is better geared to the current machine and does indeed provide exceptional performance.

6.2.2. Comparison of Architectural Differences

In addition to the impact of the operating system, other factors can affect overall algorithmic performance. For instance, one would like to compare what would happen if a faster CPU or a faster switch node were to be employed in the machine. BBN has continually updated the Butterfly family of machines from the Butterfly 1, which used MC68000 processors with 1 megabyte of memory per board, to the current generation GP1000, which uses the MC68020 with 4 megabytes of memory per board. We were not able to test the algorithms on the original Butterfly, but we were able to test them on the next generation BBN multiprocessor, the TC2000. The TC2000 is a similar design to the GP1000 but there are significant differences which are illustrated in the tables on the page following the graphs. Table 6.1 shows the difference in processor characteristics, while table 6.2 shows the difference in the memory characteristics for the GP1000 and TC2000. In general, the primary differences between the two machines are the faster CPU in the TC2000, as well as a change in the basic switch node component from a 4 x 4 crossbar to an 8 x 8 crossbar.

Table 6.1: Comparison of BBN multiprocessor CPU characteristics

Machine	CPU	Clock Speed	MIPS	MFLOPS
GP1000	M68020	16 Mhz	2.5	0.6
TC2000	M88100	20 Mhz	19	20

The faster CPU in the TC2000 necessitates a faster switch with increased path width, and an 8 x 8 crossbar switch component solves this problem. One impact of the increased size of the crossbar switch

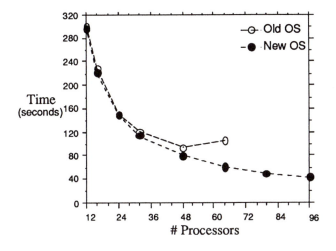

Figure 6.13: Comparison of old OS vs. new OS for mountain image, rectangular region UD

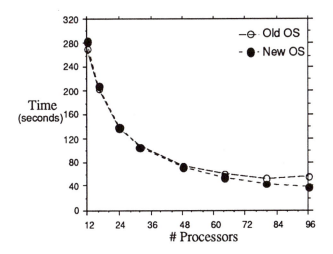

Figure 6.14: Comparison of old OS vs. new OS for mountain image, rectangular region LC

is that fewer wires are needed between the switch columns in the interconnection network. The 8 x 8 crossbar is more costly to produce than the 4 x 4 but it does allow 8 simultaneous messages to be output, whereas a 4 x 4 only supports 4 messages at a time.

Table 6.2: Comparison of BBN multiprocessor memory characteristics

Machine	Cache	Memory per Board	Switch Speed	Path Width	Basic Switch Node
GP1000	no	4 meg	8 Mhz	4 bit	4 x 4
TC2000	yes	4 or 16 meg	38 Mhz	8 bit	8 x 8

From the programmer's point of view, the TC2000 is functionally the same as the GP1000. There are several small differences regarding communication, however. The GP1000 supports the block transfer mechanism in hardware, whereby a path is held open long enough for 256 byte length messages to go from one board to another. In the TC2000, this operation is supported through software emulation rather than hardware implementation. The TC2000 does contain a memory cache which allows data to be allocated as cachable or non-cachable. Although using the cache significantly enhances performance, judicious management of this memory is required by the programmer since no cache coherence scheme is supported. The primary goal here is to compare the different algorithms under different CPU and switch characteristics, so the algorithms were not modified to take advantage of the cache.

The results, including times for the setup phase from the front end plus the tiling time, are shown in figures 6.15, 6.16, 6.17, and 6.18. A thorough analysis of the scan line algorithm was deemed unnecessary on the TC2000 due to its performance limitations noticed on the GP1000. It is, however, included for comparison purposes in the next section of this chapter.

These graphs indicate similar performance in the algorithms when compared to the previous graphs for the GP1000. The only problem with this comparison is that the results on the TC2000 were limited for most of the tests to a maximum of 48 processors, while with the GP1000, 96 processors were consistently available.[2]

---

[2]We have included some data obtained on the TC2000 at 96 processors in table 6.3. In general, though, due to the other users on the machine, only 48 processors were used for most of the tests.

TC2000 Tiling + Setup Time Comparisons

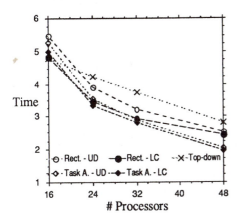

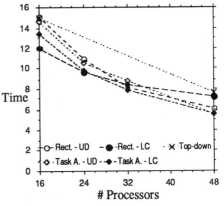

Figure 6.15: TC2000 algorithm comparison, stegosaurus image

Figure 6.17: TC2000 algorithm comparison, tree image

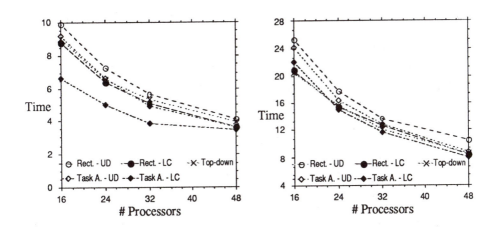

Figure 6.16: TC2000 algorithm comparison, Laser image

Figure 6.18: TC2000 algorithm comparison, mountain image

In order to allow a fair comparison between the two machines, the speedup was computed for each of the algorithms at 96 processors. The task adaptive algorithm is used for this comparison, and the results are shown in table 6.3.

Table 6.3: GP1000 and TC2000 speedup and time ratio comparison using 96 processors

Machine	Stegosaurus	Laser	Tree	Mountain
GP1000 Speedup	70.3	73.3	68.1	82.1
TC2000 Speedup	61.3	59.3	56.4	70.6
Ratio of Execution Times at $P = 96$: GP1000/TC2000	8.6	8.7	8.0	8.8

As can be seen from the table, the TC2000 exhibits slightly reduced speedup when compared to the GP1000 on 96 processors for most of the images. This could be caused by a number of factors, ranging from the amount of work per task to the processor-to-switch speed ratio. The last row in the table indicates the ratio of parallel execution times of the TC2000 divided by the GP1000. From this data, it appears that on 96 processors, the TC2000 is approximately 8.5 times faster than the GP1000 for this problem.

6.2.3. Relationship of Machine Parameters to Performance

In this section, we evaluate the various overheads on both machines to see their differences. The comparison involves examining the total processor-time space and comparing the results on the two machines. Here, the overheads are evaluated with respect to P and comparison values are shown to the right of each graph for the overhead percentages at 48 processors. Also, the speedup is given at each processor configuration. All of the algorithms are compared on the GP1000 and the TC2000 for the Laser image as a representative example. Due to the volume of data and the CPU time involved in the tests, only one image was used for comparison. Different results would be obtained for the different test images, but the main interest here was to evaluate the trend in performance and directly compare the percentages on various processor configurations.

6.2.3.1. Comparison of Overheads

The next five pages provide a direct comparison of the overhead factors for all of the algorithms. The graphs include the total processor-time space for each particular processor configuration, with the overheads clearly marked as a percentage. Although the results were measured up to 96 processors for the GP1000, the overhead values given on the right side of the graph are for 48 processors so they can be compared to the values for the TC2000 below.

6.2.3.2. Analysis

These results present a number of interesting phenomena not noticed in any previous graphs. In the parallel scan line algorithm, the latency and code modification overheads constitute almost the same overhead percentage regardless of the processor configuration on both machines. This makes sense since the number of tasks is constant regardless of the number of processors in this algorithm. In the other cases, since the total number of tasks increases with the number of processors, the overhead effects increase as well. In some cases, the load balancing may go down at some point but this may be due to an increase in another factor as explained next.

With the exception of the task adaptive algorithm, the load balancing is better on the TC2000 than in the GP1000. On the other hand, the network contention, code modification, and latency/communication are significantly worse. It seems that the increased delay due to communication overheads and contention contribute to even out the load in the algorithms on the TC2000 (recall that load balancing cannot be measured independently from other factors). Since these overheads are larger in the TC2000 than in the GP1000, they contribute to an increase in the average task execution time. This changes the load balancing since it is based on dynamic scheduling of the tasks, as well as their execution time.

In the case of the task adaptive algorithm, the load balancing is a direct result of dynamic task partitioning, and it is possible that the tasks cannot be partitioned near the end of the computation due to the imposed threshold. This effect may be more pronounced in the TC2000 than in the GP1000 due to the difference in the synchronization and communication mechanisms.

Comparison of Overhead Factors, GP1000 vs. TC2000, Laser Image, Scan line Algorithm

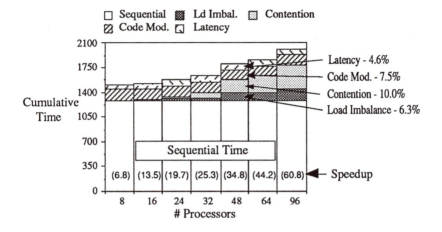

Figure 6.19: GP1000, scan line algorithm, UD, overhead comparison

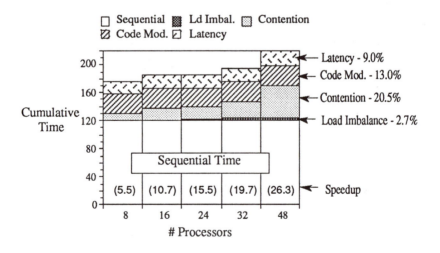

Figure 6.20: TC2000, scan line algorithm, UD, overhead comparison

Comparison of Overhead Factors, GP1000 vs. TC2000, Laser Image, Rectangular Region Algorithm, UD Scheme

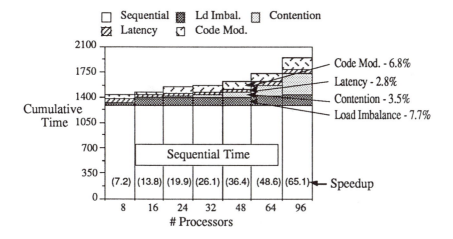

Figure 6.21: GP1000, rectangular region algorithm, UD, overhead comparison

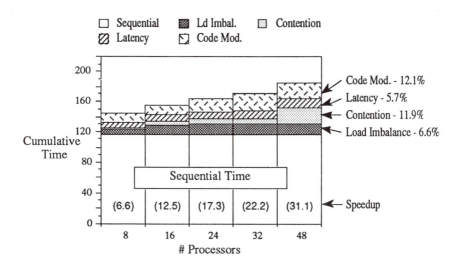

Figure 6.22: TC2000, rectangular region algorithm, UD, overhead comparison

Comparison of Overhead Factors, GP1000 vs. TC2000, Laser Image, Rectangular Region Algorithm, LC Scheme

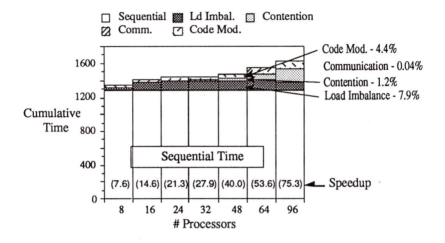

Figure 6.23: GP1000, rectangular region algorithm, LC, overhead comparison

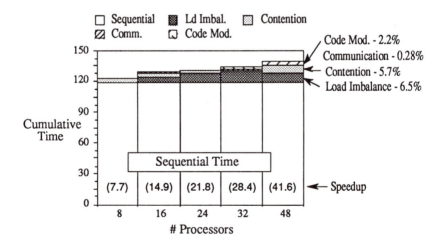

Figure 6.24: TC2000, rectangular region algorithm, LC, overhead comparison

Comparison of Overhead Factors, GP1000 vs. TC2000, Laser Image, Top-Down Algorithm

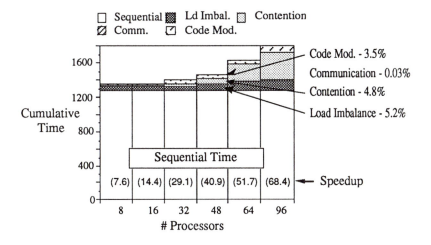

Figure 6.25: GP1000, top-down algorithm, LC, overhead comparison

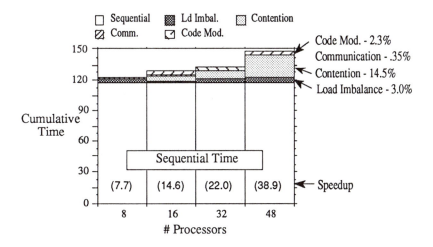

Figure 6.26: TC2000, top-down algorithm, LC, overhead comparison

Comparison of Overhead Factors, GP1000 vs. TC2000, Laser Image, Task Adaptive Algorithm

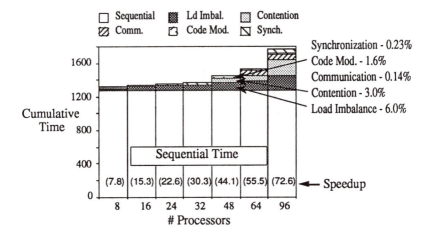

Figure 6.27: GP1000, task adaptive algorithm, LC, overhead comparison

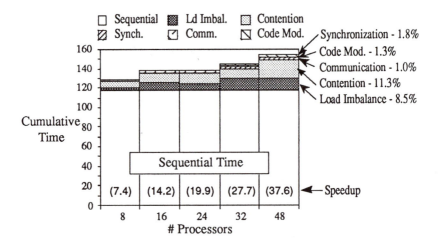

Figure 6.28: TC2000, task adaptive algorithm, LC, overhead comparison

The probable cause for the general network contention increase in the TC2000 over the GP1000 could be attributed to these factors:

1. The increase in switch speed in the TC2000 over the GP1000 does not match the corresponding increase in processor speed, therefore more collisions in the network switch are likely to occur.

2. The hardware support for block transfers in the GP1000 is not available in the TC2000 (this was used in the LC scheme).

It seems likely that the cause for the general network contention increase could be a combination of both of these reasons, especially for the LC scheme which extensively uses the block transfer mechanism. Although the TC2000 contains a cache as well as support for use of fine grained interleaved shared memory, neither of these characteristics is used in the implementation of the algorithms. The cache does not affect performance in the LC schemes, however, since the remote data is copied to local memory, where it is then cached as local data. In addition, the fine grain interleaving is not needed and would not provide better performance anyway since the shared data is already scattered among the memory modules. In the next section, the effect of enhancing the characteristics of computer graphics scenes is analyzed to determine the overall performance differential.

6.3. Scene Characteristics

One of the reasons different images are used for performance comparisons throughout this book is that it is desirable to be able to generalize these results to apply to all computer generated scenes. Of course this is an impossible task since there are always pathological cases one cannot predict. In the experiments four scenes were used which have different characteristics in screen area projection, number of data elements, and depth complexity. In this section, these same four scenes are analyzed, along with several new ones which have added scene complexity in one form or another. These break down into two categories: image complexity and object complexity .

In his thesis, Whelan analyzes several scenes which vary in complexity in terms of both of the above categories. His conclusions merely represent what most researchers intuitively realize, but they are worth repeating here:

1. Scenes are not usually composed of uniformly distributed polygons.

2. As the number of polygons increases, their size generally decreases. Somescenes may have a few large polygons which take up a significant portion of the drawn area on the screen.
3. Most polygons have few edges.
4. The aspect ratio of polygons is non-uniform, although some scenes seem to be oriented towards a particular direction.
5. The depth complexity of most pixels is fairly small (less than six), although some scenes obviously violate this rule.

It is not necessary to repeat Whelan's analysis for the scenes used here since it does not categorize scenes in terms of their difficulty in the various rendering stages. His analysis does point out that non-uniformity in scenes is the norm, so a parallel graphics algorithm must take this into account and perform well under various circumstances. The algorithms presented in this book are general purpose and are designed to handle various input scenes rather than a specific type. One cannot categorically draw a relationship between a given algorithm and say, the depth complexity of an image. Even if this were the case, does that information provide anything useful to the user community? In general, the algorithm should perform well on all imagery and should have the capability of handling pathological cases with some efficiency. This is more useful than algorithm analysis based upon depth complexity, polygon area coverage, or some other factor.

In the following sections, the different algorithms' performance is compared using an increase in image complexity in the first subsection and an increase in object complexity in the second subsection.

6.3.1. Image Complexity

Image complexity refers to the addition of features to a scene to make a higher quality image. Such additional features can include: rendering at higher resolution, advanced anti-aliasing, texture mapping, shadow generation, and bump mapping to name a few. Texturing, shadowing, or bump mapping, have not been implemented here since these features require careful planning in order to be implemented efficiently in parallel. This is primarily due to the additional memory required for each of these features, plus the desire to avoid contention for this memory. Anti-aliasing has already been incorporated into this algorithm, and all of the data presented so far includes this feature. Therefore, increasing spatial resolution is concentrated on here, and a comparison of the other features is left for future work.

All of the previous scenes are re-tested at double resolution (1280 x 968) to evaluate the performance of the different algorithms under these conditions. The first set of graphs involves a comparison similar to the others in this chapter, in which the setup phase as well as the tiling time is taken into account. The speedup and efficiency are given in the second set of graphs.

As a representative example of the times for the high resolution computations, the results for the mountain image are shown in figures 6.29 and 6.30, but the graphs for all the images are included in the appendix in figures A.21 through A.28. These graphs are zoomed in to show more detail at the higher processor counts. The speedup for the mountain image on the GP1000 using the task adaptive algorithm is shown in figure 6.31, and the efficiency for this image in figure 6.32. Since communication is the same as before but there is an increase in work due to the increased resolution, the algorithms are more efficient. Table 6.4 shows the speedup and efficiency for each of the images when calculated at high resolution on the GP1000, versus normal resolution using the task adaptive (LC) algorithm.

Table 6.4: Tiling section comparison of speedup and efficiency for normal resolution images vs. high resolution images on GP1000, 96 Processors

Images (#polygons)	Normal Resolution Speedup	High Resolution Speedup	Normal Resolution Efficiency	High Resolution Efficiency
Stegosaurus (9K)	71.4	86.5	0.74	0.90
Laser (46K)	73.6	80.0	0.77	0.83
Tree (106K)	70.5	84.6	0.73	0.88
Mountain (131K)	82.2	87.6	0.86	0.91

The data from the table indicates that the speedup varies widely among the images, but the single common result is that the additional work in the high resolution images provides better speedup and efficiency than in the normal resolution case. It is likely that the reason for the improved speedup is that the ratio of work to communication time has increased, thus reducing the network contention percentage.

High Resolution Tiling + FE Comparison

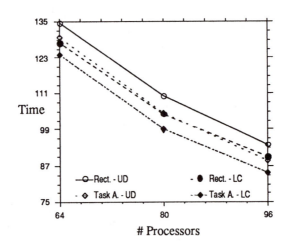

Figure 6.29: Rectangular vs. task adaptive on GP1000, mountain image, high-res

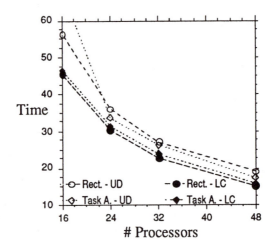

Figure 6.30: Rectangular vs. task adaptive on TC2000, mountain image, high-res

Speedup and Efficiency of High Resolution Image

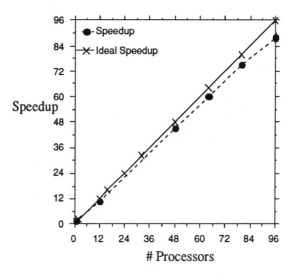

Figure 6.31: Speedup for high-res mountain image, GP1000

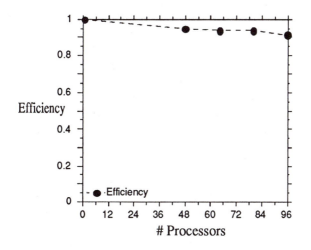

Figure 6.32: Efficiency for high-res mountain image, GP1000

This is logical since the amount of network traffic has not changed, but the amount of work has increased due to the increase in spatial resolution. In the next section, the algorithms are compared on a different set of images which involve much higher numbers of polygons to see the expected times on these datasets.

6.3.2. Object Complexity

One of the goals of this work was to present solutions for developing a highly efficient parallel rendering algorithm which allows extremely fast computation of complex imagery. To this end, new datasets are evaluated which contain a considerably greater number of polygons. Examples of two highly complex datasets are the rings image in color plate 5 and the dense tree image shown in color plate 6. The dense tree image has more polygons than the previously evaluated tree image, particularly in the twigs. Due to the amount of memory required for the tree dataset, it is not possible to evaluate speedup and efficiency since not enough physical memory was available even locally. All of the images are evaluated based on their total time, as well as the number of polygons rendered per second. Hardware manufacturers typically quote a figure of polygons per second in evaluating hardware Z-buffer graphics workstations. A typical example of this type of machine is the HP-320/SRX. Some of the images which were evaluated previously have been rendered on this machine by Eric Haines, who developed the SPD database from which the tree, mountain, and rings datasets were extracted. Table 6.5 shows a comparison of all the images and the effective number of polygons per second achieved. These results were obtained using the task adaptive algorithm on 96 processors of a BBN TC2000.

In comparison to the values in the table, Haines ran some of the same tests on the HP-320/SRX [Hain87b]. In rendering the dense tree, 4835 polygons/second was achieved. Using a denser version of the rings image (874 K polygons) than employed here, the HP-320/SRX achieved 4819 polygons/second. For comparison, a current example of a state of the art graphics superworkstation is the Silicon Graphics Iris 4D VGX [Haeb90]. The manufacturer quotes a figure of 750,000 Gouraud-shaded triangles per second for this machine.

This value for the hardware performance is based on Gouraud shaded polygons which are not anti-aliased. Our data is for Phong shaded polygons with specular highlights and stochastic sampled anti-aliasing. Although it is difficult to compare exactly, the addition of Phong shading typically might cost 3 times as much as Gouraud shading, in addition to the anti-aliasing cost which is about 4 times as

Table 6.5: Effective rendering rate and speedup using 96 processors on BBN TC2000, task adaptive algorithm

Images	# Polygons	Time (sec.)	Polygons/Second	Speedup
Stegosaurus	9,639	1.14	8,455	61.3
Laser	46,393	2.02	22,967	59.3
Tree	106,289	2.94	32,907	56.4
Mountain	131,072	4.12	29,857	70.6
Rings	567,841	9.90	52,239	85.6
Dense Tree	851,288	8.81	80,690	58.9

much for stochastic sampling as it is for a Z-buffer. Also, the amount of physical memory required to support over 500,000 polygons is most likely not available within a graphics workstation, and this will almost certainly slow down the hardware. Nevertheless, the results given here are significantly faster than a slightly older generation graphics workstation and might compare favorably with a current generation machine. When the fact that the rendering is done in software rather than hardware in this algorithm is added, the benefit is that much greater since the software version allows much more flexibility in its use. This is elaborated upon in the next chapter.

6.4. Conclusions

Based on all of the data reported in this chapter, it seems clear that the task adaptive algorithm utilizing the LC memory referencing scheme provides the best performance for all types of imagery among the methods implemented. Besides performance, other advantages of the task adaptive approach are:

1. It is unnecessary to determine an initial optimal granularity ratio for this algorithm. The number of areas chosen initially corresponds to the number of processors in the system, and high performance is achieved regardless of machine configuration. In the other algorithms, this ratio must be derived for each image independently for the best performance.

2. The load balancing in the task adaptive approach is completely dynamic, based on the amount of work left. Because of this, worst case scenarios, such as all of the data being located in one portion of the screen, can be handled effectively while the other algorithms will not perform nearly as well in this type of situation.

3. This approach has minimal time cost in the setup phase of the front end since the number of areas is very small initially. Hence, this time is much less than in the other algorithms.

In summary, the first section of this chapter presents an analysis of several different memory referencing strategies. Based on this theoretical analysis, the Uniformly Distributed and Locally Cached schemes are shown to only differ by several tenths of a second. A description regarding the implementation of both of these schemes is then presented in detail. After comparing the results of the implementations, it is clear that the LC scheme combined with the task adaptive decomposition method results in the best performance for all the test imagery. The setup time from the front end for each approach is included for the timings, in order to allow a fair comparison and substantiate this fact. The theoretical analysis of the memory reference strategies indicated that there would only be a small difference between the UD and LC schemes. Instead, the difference is much larger due to the fact that network contention is not accounted for in the theoretical analysis. This contention is an important degradation factor since it is significantly smaller in the LC scheme than it is in the UD scheme.

The second section involves a comparison of the different parallel algorithms with respect to changes in the underlying machine parameters. It is shown that a change in the GP1000 operating system which allows parallel page faults markedly improved performance over the previous version of this operating system. When using the next generation version of the BBN multiprocessor known as the TC2000, the faster CPU and network switch improves performance in all cases almost an order of magnitude over the GP1000. The task adaptive algorithm using the LC scheme proves to be the best performer for this new machine as well. A comparison of overhead factors between the two machines reveals that network contention plays a more significant role in degrading performance in the TC2000 than in the GP1000 when measured at 48 processors, however. A possible explanation is that the interconnection network speed increase from the GP1000 to the TC2000 does not match the corresponding increase in the CPU performance. As a result, tasks execute faster, but the communication of data is more frequent, leading to a greater possibility of a blocked path in the network. The TC2000 offers enhancements to memory referencing (such as a hardware cache) that are not incorporated into the implemented algorithms. It is possible that if these are utilized, the effects of network contention could be reduced.

The third section in this chapter involves an analysis of the effect of increasing image and object complexity in the test scenes. Re-evaluating the performance of the algorithms at a resolution of 1280 x 968 on the mountain image reveals a speedup of 87.6 on 96 processors using the task adaptive algorithm on the GP1000. In addition, using a highly complex scene with over 800,000 data elements, an effective polygon rendering rate of over 80,000 anti-aliased Phong shaded polygons per second is achieved on 96 processors of a TC2000. This is most likely the fastest rendering ever realized to this point using a software algorithm on a general purpose MIMD architecture for graphics rendering.

7

Conclusion

This book has primarily concentrated on the development and analysis of various approaches to tiling three-dimensional computer generated scenes on a multiprocessor. In doing so we have presented the following:

1. A categorization of possible parallel approaches to graphics rendering into a taxonomy according to graphical task decomposition.
2. A number of methods which incorporate parallelism in all aspects of a graphics rendering program.
3. A quantitative analysis of various degradation factors encountered in a multiprocessor graphics display algorithm implementation.
4. The development of general task partitioning and memory referencing strategies which may be used in other graphics rendering algorithms, as well as non-graphics applications.

These will be described in detail in the following sections.

7.1. Summary

In the past, research in the area of parallel graphics rendering has concentrated primarily on approaches to tiling a scene. This portion of the program involves the hidden surface removal and subsequent smooth shading operations necessary to establish a realistic rendering. Although this is the most time consuming portion of a graphics display program, little work has been spent on the development of parallel approaches to the front end and back end of such a program. If this is not done, the advantage gained in parallelizing the tiling portion will be lost when the other parts are executed sequentially. Although the front end and back end portions of the programs presented here were not analyzed fully, a pipelined approach was developed t speed up significantly these segments of the algorithms. In addition, these phases are well integrated with the tiling portion of the programs, thus providing a general purpose high performance approach to parallel rendering which could be used in real-world applications. This means that the parallel programs presented here will provide faster speed than other programs developed in the past which do not incorporate parallelism into the non-tiling phases.

The results in chapter 6 indicate that the task adaptive algorithm maintains the highest performance of the image space algorithms which were implemented. By splitting tasks into areas dynamically, the maximum amount of coherence is maintained in this approach. The setup time in the front end is small since the number of areas created initially is reduced in comparison to the other approaches. This is due to the fact that the initial number of areas chosen is equal to the number of processors currently available in the system. The added advantage here is that it is unnecessary to find an optimal granularity ratio prior to tiling the scene, as opposed to the other algorithmic approaches. Another advantage of this scheme is that worst case situations, such as a high concentration of data in a small portion of the image, are handled elegantly and will not present a problem. This algorithm, when combined with the Locally Cached memory referencing scheme, offers the best overall performance on the tested datasets. In addition, based on the timings shown in both chapter 5 and chapter 6, the algorithm performs well all the way up to 96 processors on both Butterfly multiprocessors. An efficiency of over 90% was obtained with the mountain image on 96 processors on the GP1000. In addition, using the rings database which contains over 500,000 polygons, an efficiency of 84% was obtained on the TC2000 computer. This indicates that parallel processing of computer graphics rendering is a cost effective solution for use with very complex datasets.

Based on the data presented in this book, it seems that the less complicated approaches to parallel decomposition obtain the highest performance. Many researchers have challenged this notion by developing complicated solutions to the parallel rendering problem. While this may be necessary in a hardware environment, it usually compromises performance in the software environment due to the extra overheads of synchronization, etc. The simple techniques presented here for dynamic task decomposition, along with judicious memory management schemes, combine to solve the problem in a straightforward manner.

One common misconception that might be perceived regarding parallel display algorithms is that when graphical coherence is lost, performance will suffer greatly. Indeed, coherence has played a significant role in enhancing the development of serial display algorithms. In a parallel context, however, even when a large number (2,304) of areas is created, the overhead is limited to only about 6% of the total execution time. Clearly, an approach which uses groups of small scan line areas reduces the overhead due to coherence. The loss due to lack of coherence is not as great as one might think, so parallel processing of areas does not add significant overhead to the serial approaches developed in the past.

In general, other factors play a more important role than coherence in the performance of the parallel algorithms. Most of the degradation relates to either load balancing or communication. One of the important facts brought out here is that an algorithm which strictly emphasizes load balancing does not guarantee the best performance. This is shown in the times for the data adaptive algorithm. This algorithm does exhibit the least amount of overhead due to load imbalance; however, the implementation of this approach forces additional overhead to be incurred in other parts of the algorithm that negate the gains achieved by a balanced load.

Memory usage also plays an important role in a number of ways. The Uniformly Distributed (UD) memory referencing scheme introduces latency, while the Locally Cached (LC) memory referencing scheme requires communication using block transfers. As a result of the large volume of message traffic due to retrieving data in the UD scheme, a significant amount of network contention is introduced. The LC scheme minimizes this factor, but it still plays an important role in the degradation in performance, especially on large processor configurations. Network contention is difficult to predict since it is related to the number of requests for paths in the interconnection network at a given time. When the interval between requests is large, the contention is small, and vice versa. This explains why an analytical model that does not relate network contention to communication in the system will not accurately predict performance. Although researchers have developed a good model [Nand90] for computation in this type of environment, it is difficult to use in the context of a complex algorithm such as this one. The task adaptive algorithm uses larger tasks which require communication less frequently than the other approaches, except toward the end of the computation. Contention is not reduced in this approach, though, since the issue of how to limit the burst of communication at the end of the computation due to the large amount of task splitting has not been fully addressed.

The Butterfly interconnect is an example of a high speed network, but contention still plays an important role in the algorithms shown here. This should be taken into account in the implementation of any program involving a large amount of data movement. The problem of network contention can be resolved if the usage of the network is reduced or more switch paths are made available in the hardware. The latter is not usually a solution available to the programmer, so the former approach must be taken. This was used in the LC memory referencing strategy which was developed solely for the purpose of limiting communication in the system. Further refinements of this scheme could be added to reduce the number and size of the messages, particularly in the case of the task adaptive algorithm.

The following generalizations can be made regarding implementations on parallel machines of algorithms with high data movement, such as the ones developed here. The memory referencing strategy directly affects performance in the system since it is directly related to the communication of data. The frequency and amount of communication determines the overall degradation due to network contention. Any reduction of this factor is certain to provide high performance, especially in applications where there is a large dataset requiring frequent referencing. Another point is that global scattering of data among the memory modules in a shared memory NUMA machine is necessary to counteract the problem of hot spot contention. Using some type of caching scheme to bring in data to the local memory module prior to referencing is crucial to high performance since it minimizes network traffic and reduces latency. Finally, the coarsest granularity for tasks which allows adequate load balancing is the best approach to take in order to achieve good parallel timings. The graphs of granularity ratio versus overhead effects (figures A.5, A.6, A.7, and A.8) show that other overhead factors are increased when the granularity becomes too fine. As an example, the task adaptive approach uses the smallest number of tasks to minimize these effects in comparison to the other decompositions.

From the results presented herein, it can be seen that high performance can be achieved in a graphics display algorithm on a parallel architecture. Since graphics applications tend to be data intensive, the memory must be managed effectively, something which has not been done in some parallel graphics algorithms developed in the past. Other graphics applications such as volume rendering, image processing, and radiosity can take advantage of some of the techniques described here for use in a parallel environment. For instance, the LC memory referencing scheme could be modified for usage in each of these instances since the data to be rendered for a particular task is known a priori. In addition, the task adaptive algorithm could also be modified for task partitioning purposes for these rendering techniques. In addition, non-graphics applications can also utilize the techniques described here. Example applications might include geographical information systems, global climate modeling, finite element simulation, and applied graph theory.

During the development of this project, many problems were encountered when implementing the parallel algorithms on the Butterfly. Several software tools available with this machine made program development much easier than it otherwise might have been. *Gist* is a performance analysis package which shows a graph of processors versus time in an X-window display. By setting events at critical time points in the program, one can evaluate the performance of the program by looking at how long a particular phase takes to execute on each processor. The graphical output of this tool aids in the programmer's understanding of the processor-time graph. A parallel profiler is also available which can generate individual processor profiles and this is also a useful tool for evaluating program performance. The primary software tool that allows greater understanding of the internal nature of the parallel aspect of the programs is a parallel debugger called *TotalView*. Without this tool, situations like race conditions, synchronization problems, and shared memory problems would have been much more difficult to debug. This environment made program debugging, testing, and analysis an easy interactive task which hastened the development of the evaluated programs.

Even with the fact that BBN is no longer building the Butterfly, scalable shared memory multiprocessors are not dead. Clearly, latency and contention issues are the primary target areas for improvement. Tera Computer Company is designing a machine to combat both of these issues in a scalable shared memory architecture. Message passing machines seem to be growing in popularity, and it would be useful to determine how these types of machines could be used for fast graphics rendering. While the memory referencing strategies of the algorithms presented here might need to be modified for this type of machine, the work decomposition methods would not require modification. It is possible that a number of different decomposition strategies will lead to good results due to the different topologies and communication performance in these architectures. In addition, message passing architectures have distributed memory like the Butterfly so an extension of the LC memory referencing scheme might prove to be a viable solution in that environment.

The analysis and performance results given in this book should serve as a guide to the reader regarding the critical issues involved in the development of a parallel graphics rendering program. In addition, the algorithmic possibilities which are worthwhile taking into account during the development and tuning process have been presented and can certainly be modified according to the machine available to the programmer.

7.2. Future Work

There are still a number of unanswered questions which have not been addressed in this book, in addition to new questions brought out by the results reported here. Next, these are elaborated upon with regard to potential future areas of work.

In relation to machine parameters, it would be interesting to see what new issues are encountered on a very large multiprocessor containing 512 or an even greater number of processors. It is entirely possible that the algorithms will need to be changed to handle this type of situation. As the speed of microprocessors has increased over the years, the interconnection network speed has not increased as quickly. While the TC2000 network is faster than the GP1000 network, it seemed to incur greater network contention. This is most likely due to the fact that the performance of the interconnection network was not increased at the same rate that the processor speed was increased. It would be interesting to analyze this phenomenon in detail, not just for graphics algorithms, but for other applications as well. This might provide insight for hardware as well as software designers when planning a program for parallel implementation.

Another machine characteristic specifically relevant to the TC2000 is the use of the hardware cache as well as interleaved shared memory. The cache provides fast access to read-only shared data which is stored globally. On TC2000 machines which contain 16 megabytes of memory per processor, it is possible to configure a portion of the memory on each processor as fine-grained interleaved. The programmer no longer has to make sure that the data is scattered across the memory modules since it is implicitly done in this case. In addition, the granularity of interleaving is much finer than was possible before, so that even a one-dimensional array can be scattered among the memory modules. The combination of using the cache with storing read-only data in the interleaved shared memory might produce better results than the LC scheme developed in this book, but the cachable data would need to be managed effectively. This would alleviate the programmer from the burden of programming the complex code necessary to implement the LC scheme.

Other researchers have investigated techniques by which the operating system manages the storage and access of shared memory in an NUMA architecture such as the Butterfly [Laro90]. This level of management by the operating system allows use of a memory referencing method such as the UD scheme which is easy to develop, while the operating system manages the location and storage of data and attempts to optimize it for high program performance.

Other future work in developing parallel graphics display algorithms might look at different implementations of memory referencing schemes, investigate methods to alleviate communication, and look at the handling of even larger graphics datasets. Graphics features such as shadows, texture maps, bump maps, and motion blur also present interesting challenges to a parallel implementation. Each of these features requires additional memory, and the use of the memory in some cases cannot be localized. For instance, texture mapping requires referencing a two-dimensional array of pixel values to assign a more detailed property to a particular polygon or object. If the map is scattered throughout memory, hot spot contention will be minimized, but memory latency will occur. A caching technique like the LC scheme could be used to bring in the portion of the map that is relevant for a particular polygon or object. This method might require a very large portion of the texture, and there may not be enough local processor memory to facilitate this type of approach. Another enhancement which might be worth investigating in the future involves fast update of small scenes in real-time. In fact, this is the type of work that is currently being investigated for scientific visualization at Lawrence Livermore National Lab. We hope to report on the success of this project in the future.

References

[ABRA86]   Abram, G. *Parallel Image Generation with Anti-Aliasing and Texturing*, Ph.D. dissertation, University of North Carolina at Chapel Hill, 1986.

[AHUJ86]   Ahuja, S.; Carriero, N.; and Gelernter, D. "Linda and Friends." *IEEE Computer 19*, 8 (August 1986) pp. 26-34.

[ALLI91]   Allison, M. Private communication, July, 1991.

[AMDA67]   Amdahl, G. "Validity of the Single-Processor Approach to Achieving Large-Scale Computer Capabilities." *AFIPS Conference Proceedings 30*(1967) pp. 483-485.

[APGA88]   Apgar, B.; Bersack, B.; and Mammen, A. "A Display System for the Stellar Graphics Supercomputer Model GS1000." *Computer Graphics, Proceedings of Siggraph 22*, 4 (August 1988) pp. 255-262.

[ARVI86]   Arvind and Ianucci, R.A. "Two Fundamental Issues in Multiprocessing. "Tech. Rept. 226-4, MIT Laboratory of Computer Science, Cambridge, Massachusetts, March, 1986.

[BADO90]   Badouel, D.; Bouatouch, K.; and Priol, T. "Ray Tracing on Distributed Memory Parallel Computers: Strategies for Distributing Computations and Data." *Course Notes for Course 28, Siggraph* (1990) pp. 185-198.

[BAUM90]   Baum, D.R. and Winget, J.M. "Real Time Radiosity Through Parallel Processing and Hardware Acceleration," *Computer Graphics 24*, 2, (March 1990) pp. 67-75.

[BBN84]   BBN Laboratories, Inc. *Development of a Butterfly Multiprocessor Test Bed, The Butterfly Switch*, July, 1984, Report No. 5874.

[BBN89A]   BBN Advanced Computers, Inc. *Programming in C with the Uniform System*, 1989.

[BBN89B]   BBN Advanced Computers, Inc. *Butterfly GP1000 Switch Tutorial*, March, 1989.

[BERM87]   Berman, F. and Snyder, L. "On Mapping Parallel Algorithms into Parallel Architectures." *Journal of Parallel and Distributed Computing* 4(1987).

[BLIN77]   Blinn, J.F. "Models of Light Reflection for Computer Synthesized Pictures." *Computer Graphics, Proceedings of Siggraph* 11(1977) pp. 192-198.

[BURK90]   Burke, A. and Leler, W. "Parallelism and Graphics: An Introduction and Annotated Bibliography." *Course Notes for Siggraph Course 28, ACM Siggraph Conference* (1990) pp. 111-140.

[CARP84]   Carpenter, L.C. "The A-Buffer, an Anti-Aliased Hidden Surface Method." *Computer Graphics, Proceedings of Siggraph* 18, 3 (1984) pp. 103-108.

[CASP89]   Caspary, E. and Scherson, I.D. "A self-balanced parallel ray-tracing algorithm," in *Parallel Processing for Computer Vision and Display*, P.M. Dew, T.R. Heywood, and R.A. Earnshaw, editors, Addison-Wesley, 1989, pp. 408-419.

[CATM74]   Catmull, E. *A Subdivision Algorithm for Computer Display of Curved Surfaces*, Ph.D. dissertation, NTIS A004 968, University of Utah, December 1974.

[CHAL91]   Challinger, J. "Parallel Volume Rendering on a Shared Memory Multiprocessor." UCSC-CRL-91-23, University of California, Santa Cruz, 1991.

[CHAN81]   Chang, P. and Jain, R. "A Multi-Processor System for Hidden Surface Removal." *Computer Graphics* 15, 4 (December 1981) pp.405-436.

[CHEN88]   Chen, M.C. "Mapping Parallel Algorithms onto General-Purpose Parallel Machines." *Proceedings of the 21st Annual Hawaii International Conference on System Sciences 1*(1988).

[CLEA83]   Cleary, J.G;, Wyvill, B.M.; Birtwistle, G.M;, and Vatti, R. "Multiprocessor Ray Tracing." Tech. Rept. 83/128/17, University of Calgary, 1983.

[COOK82]   Cook, R.L. and Torrance, K.E. "A Reflectance Model for Computer Graphics." *ACM Transactions on Graphics 1*(1982) pp. 7-24.

[COOK86]   Cook, R.L. "Stochastic Sampling in Computer Graphics." *ACM Transactions on Graphics* (January 1986).

[COOP87]   Cooper, E.C. and Draves, R.P. "C Threads." Internal Research note of the Mach Project, Carnegie Mellon University, April, 1987.

[CROC91]   Crockett, T.W. and Orloff, T. "A Parallel Rendering Algorithm for MIMD Architectures," ICASE Tech. Rept. No. 91-3, NASA Langley Research Center, June, 1991.

[CROW77]   Crow, F.C. "Shadow Algorithms for Computer Graphics." *Computer Graphics, Proceedings of Siggraph 11*, 3 (July 1977) pp. 242-248.

[CROW88A]   Crow, F.C. "Parallelism in Rendering Algorithms." *Proceedings of Graphics Interface* (June 1988).

[CROW88B]   Crow, F.C; Demos, G.; Hardy, J.; McLaughlin, J.; and Sims, K. "3D Image Synthesis on the Connection Machine." *Proceedings of the International Conference on Parallel Processing for Computer Vision and Display* (January 1988), Leeds, UK.

[DEER88]   Deering, M.; Winner, S.; Schediwy, B.; Duffy, C.; and Hunt, N. "The Triangle Processor and Normal Vector Shader: A VLSI System for High Performance Graphics." *Computer Graphics, Proceedings of Siggraph 22*, 4 (August 1988).

[DIED88]   Diede, T.; Hagenmaier, C.F.; Miranker, G.S.; Rubinstein, J.; and Worley, W.S. Jr. "The Titan Graphics Supercomputer Architecture." *IEEE Computer* (September 1988).

[DYER87]   Dyer, S. and Whitman, S. "A Vectorized Scan line Z-Buffer Rendering Algorithm." *IEEE Computer Graphics & Applications 7*, 7 (July 1987) pp. 34-45.

[FIUM83]   Fiume, E.; Fournier, A.; and Rudolph, L. "A Parallel Scan Conversion Algorithm with Anti-Aliasing for a General Purpose Ultracomputer." *Computer Graphics, Proceedings of Siggraph 17*, 3 (July 1983) pp. 141-149.

[FRAN80]   Franklin, W.R. "A Linear Time Exact Hidden Surface Algorithm." *Computer Graphics, Proceedings of Siggraph 14*, 3 (1980) pp. 117-123.

[FRAN90]   Franklin, W.R. and Kankanhalli, M.S. "Parallel Object-Space Hidden Surface Removal." *Computer Graphics, Proceedings of Siggraph 24*, 4 (August 1990) pp. 87-94.

[FUCH79]   Fuchs, H. and Johnson, B.W. "An Expandable Multiprocessor Architecture for Video Graphics." *Proceedings of the 6th Annual ACM-IEEE Symposium on Computer Architecture* (1979) pp. 58-67.

[FUCH85]   Fuchs, H.; Goldfeather, J.; Hultquist, J.P; Spach S.; Austin, J.D.; Brooks, F.P. Jr.; Eyles, J.G.; and Poulton, J. "Fast Spheres, Shadows, Textures, Transparencies, and Image Enhancements in Pixel-Planes." *Computer Graphics, Proceedings of Siggraph 19*, 3 (July 1985) pp. 111-120.

[FUCH89]   Fuchs, H.; Poulton, J.; Eyles, J.; Greer, T.; Goldfeather, J.; Ellsworth, D.; Molnar, S.; Turk, G.; Tebbs, B.; and Israel, L. "Pixel-Planes 5: A Heterogeneous Multiprocessor Graphics System Using Processor-Enhanced Memories." *Computer Graphics, Proceedings of Siggraph 23*, 3 (July 1989) pp. 79-88.

[GARL90]   Garlick, B.J.; Winget, J.M.; and Baum, D.R. "Interactive Viewing of Large Geometric Databases Using Multiprocessor Graphics Workstations," *Parallel Algorithms and Architectures for 3D Image Generation, Siggraph Course 28*, August, 1990.

[GHAR88]   Gharachorloo, N.; Gupta, S.; Hokenek, E.; Balasubramanian, P.; Bogholtz, B.; Mathieu, C.; and Zoulas, C. "Subnanosecond Pixel Rendering with Million Transistor Chips." *Computer Graphics, Proceedings of Siggraph 22*, 4 (August 1988).

[GHOS86]   Ghosal, D. and Patnaik, L.M. "Parallel Polygon Scan Conversion Algorithms: Performance Evaluation of a Shared Bus Architecture." *Computers & Graphics 10*, 1 (1986) pp. 7-25.

[GORD91]   Gorda, B.; Warren, K.; and Brooks, E.D. III "Programming in PCP," Tech. Rept. UCRL-MA-107029, Lawrence Livermore National Laboratory, April, 1991.

[GOTT83]   Gottlieb, A.; Grishman, R.; Kruskal, C.P.; McAuliffe, K.P.; Rudolph, L.; and Snir, M. "The NYU Ultracomputer - Designing an MIMD Shared Memory Parallel Computer." *IEEE Transactions on Computers C-32*, 2 (February 1983) pp. 175-189.

[GOUR71]   Gouraud, H. "Continuous Shading of Curved Surfaces." *IEEE Transactions on Computers C-20* (June 1971) pp. 623-629.

[GREE89]   Green, S. and Paddon, D. "Exploiting Coherence for Multiprocessor Ray Tracing." *IEEE Computer Graphics and Applications 9*, 6 (November 1989) pp. 12-26.

[HAEB90]   Haeberli, P. and Akeley, K. "The Accumulation Buffer: Hardware Support for High-Quality Rendering." *Computer Graphics, Proceedings of Siggraph 24*, 4 (August 1990) pp. 309-318.

[HAIN87A]   Haines, E. "A Proposal for Standard Graphics Environments." *IEEE Computer Graphics & Applications 7*, 11 (November 1987) pp. 3-5.

[HAIN87B]   Haines, E. *Standard Procedural Database Documentation,* Unpublished, 1987.

[HU85]   Hu, M.-C. and Foley, J.D. "Parallel Processing Approaches to Hidden-Surface Removal in Image Space." *Computers & Graphics 9,* 3 (1985) pp. 93-317.

[JAMI87]   Jamieson, L.H. *Characteristics of Parallel Algorithms,* MIT Press (1987) pp. 65-100.

[KAPL79]   Kaplan, M. and Greenberg, D.P. "Parallel Processing Techniques for Hidden Surface Removal." *Computer Graphics, Proceedings of Siggraph 13,* 2 (July 1979) pp. 300-307.

[KIRK90]   Kirk, D. and Voorhies, D. "The Rendering Architecture of the DN10000VS." *Computer Graphics, Proceedings of Siggraph 24,* 4 (August 1990) pp. 299-307.

[KUCK86]   Kuck, D.J.; Davidson, E.S.; Lawrie, D.H.; and Sameh, A.H. "Parallel Supercomputing Today and the Cedar Approach." *Science 231*(February 1986) pp. 967-974.

[KUMA86]   Kumar, M. and Pfister, G.F. "The Onset of Hot Spot Contention." *Proceedings of the 1986 International Conference on Parallel Processing* (1986) pp. 28-34.

[LARO90]   LaRowe, R.P. Jr. and Ellis, C.S. "Experimental Comparison of Memory Management Policies for NUMA Multiprocessors." Tech. Rept. CS-1990-10, Duke University, Durham, NC, April, 1990.

[MYER75]   Myers, A. J. "An Efficient Visible Surface Program." Tech. Rept. The Ohio State University Computer Graphics Research Group, July, 1975.

[NAND90]   Nanda, A.K; Shing, H.; Tzen, T.-H.; and Ni, L.M. "A Replicate Workload Framework to Study Performance Degradation in Shared-Memory Multiprocessors." *Proceedings of the International Conference on Parallel Processing* (1990) pp. I-161 to I-168.

[NITZ91]   Nitzburg, B. and Lo, V. "Distributed Shared Memory: A Survey of Issues and Algorithms," *Computer 24,* 8 (August 1991), pp. 52-60.

[NUGE88]   Nugent, S.F. "The iPSC/2 Direct-Connect Communications Technology." *Proceedings of the Third Hypercube Conference, ACM* (1988).

[PARE88]   Parent, R.E. and Klasky, R.S. "Using Object Clusters for Efficient Calculation of Computer Generated Images." Tech. Rept. OSU-CISRC-TR39, The Ohio State University, Columbus, Ohio, December, 1988.

[PARK80]   Parke, F.I. "Simulation and Expected Performance Analysis of Multiple Processor Z-Buffer Systems." *Computer Graphics, Proceedings of Siggraph 14*, 3 (July 1980) pp. 48-56.

[PHON75]   Phong, B.T. "Illumination for Computer Generated Pictures." *Communications of the ACM 18*, 6 (June 1975) pp. 311-317.

[PLUN85]   Plunkett, D.J. and Bailey, M.J. "The Vectorization of a Ray-Tracing Algorithm for Improved Execution Speed." *IEEE Computer Graphics & Applications 5*, 8 (August 1985) pp. 52-60.

[POTM89]   Potmesil, M. and Hoffert, E.M. "The Pixel Machine: A Parallel Image Computer." *Computer Graphics, Proceedings of Siggraph 23*, 3 (July 1989) pp. 69-78.

[RAO89]   Rao, V.N. and Kumar, V. "Parallel Depth First Search." *International Journal of Parallel Programming 16*, 6 (1989).

[ROBL88]   Roble, D.R. "A Load Balanced Parallel Scan line Z-Buffer Algorithm for the iPSC Hypercube." In *Proceedings of Pixim '88,* Paris, France, October 1988.

[ROGE85]   Rogers, D. *Procedural Elements for Computer Graphics,* McGraw-Hill (1985).

[SADA87]   Sadayappan, P. and Ercal, F. "Nearest Neighbor Mapping of Finite Element Graphs onto Processor Meshes." *IEEE Transactions on Computers 36*, 12 (December 1987).

[SADA88]   Sadayappan, P. and Visvanathan, V. "Circuit Simulation on Shared-Memory Multiprocessors." *IEEE Transactions on Computers 37*, 12 (December 1988).

[SAMI89]   Samiotakis, I. *A Thread Library for a Non Uniform Memory Access Multiprocessor*, Master's thesis, The Ohio State University, Columbus, Ohio, 1989.

[SCHR91]   Schröder, P.and Salem, J.B. "Fast Rotation of Volume Data on Data Parallel Architectures," Tech. Rept. TMC-195, Thinking Machines Corporation. (Also available in *Course Notes for Advance Volume Visualization Course, Siggraph* (1991) as well as *Visualization '91 Proceedings*, San Diego, CA, Oct. 1991.)

[SLAT90]   Slater, A.E. *Parallel Processing in Computer Graphics*, Master's thesis, University of Massachusetts, 1990.

[SMAL89]   Smallbone, J. "Programming high performance graphics on the DAP," in *Parallel Processing for Computer Vision and Display*, P.M. Dew, T.R. Heywood, and R.A. Earnshaw, editors, Addison-Wesley, 1989, pp. 321-328.

[SUTH74]   Sutherland, I.E.; Sproull, R. F;, and Schumacker, R.A. "A Characterization of Ten Hidden-Surface Removal Algorithms." *Computing Surveys 6*, 1 (March 1974).

[SUTH75]   Sutherland, I. *System of Polygon Sorting By Dissection*, U.S. Patent 3,889,107, 1975.

[THEO86]   Theoharis, T.A. "Exploiting Parallelism in the Graphics Pipeline." Tech. Rept. PRG-54, Oxford University Computing Laboratory, June, 1986.

[THEO89a]   Theoharis, T. and Page, I. "Parallel incremental polygon rendering on a SIMD processor array," in *Parallel Processing for Computer Vision and Display*, P.M. Dew, T.R. Heywood, and R.A. Earnshaw, editors, Addison-Wesley, 1989, pp. 329-337.

[THEO89b]   Theoharis, T. *Algorithms for Parallel Polygon Rendering*, Springer-Verlag (1989).

[UPSO89]   Upson, C. and Fangmeier, S. "The role of visualization and parallelism in a heterogeneous supercomputing environment," in *Parallel Processing for Computer Vision and Display*, P.M. Dew, T.R. Heywood, and R.A. Earnshaw, editors, Addison-Wesley, 1989, pp. 286-297.

[WARN69]   Warnock, J.E. "A Hidden-Surface Algorithm for Computer Generated Half-tone Pictures." Tech. Rept. TR 4-15, University of Utah, NTIS AD-753 671, June, 1969.

[WATK70]   Watkins, G.S. A Real-Time Visible Surface Algorithm. Tech. Rept. UTEC-CSc-70-101, Univeristy of Utah, NTIS AD-762 004, June, 1970.

[WEIL77]   Weiler, K. and Atherton, P. "Hidden Surface Removal Using Polygon Area Sorting." *Computer Graphics, Proceedings of Siggraph 11*, 2 (1977) pp. 214-222.

[WHEL85]   Whelan, D.S. *Animac: A Multiprocessor Architecture for Real-Time Computer Animation*, Ph.D. dissertation, California Institute of Technology, 1985.

[WHIT80]   Whitted, T. "An Improved Illumination Model for Shaded Display." *Communications of the ACM 23*(1980) pp. 343-349.

[WHIT88]   Whitman, S. and Parent, R. "A Survey of Parallel Hidden Surface Removal Algorithms." *Proceedings of Pixim '88* (October 1988), Paris, France.

[WHIT89]   Whitman, S. and Guenter, B. "The Design of Image Space Graphics Display Algorithms for MIMD Architectures." *Course Notes for Siggraph Course 16, ACM Siggraph Conference* (1989) pp. 129-155.

[WHIT90]   Whitman, S. "Computer Graphics Rendering on a Parallel Processor." *Course Notes for Course 28, Siggraph* (1990) pp. 167-183.

[WHIT91]   Whitman, S. and Sadayappan, P. "Computer Graphics Rendering on a Shared Memory Multiprocessor," *Proceedings of the International Conference on Parallel Processing,* (August 1991) CRC Press, pp. 191-194.

[WILL78]   Williams, L. "Casting Curved Shadows on Curved Surfaces." *Computer Graphics, Proceedings of Siggraph 12,* 3 (July 1978) pp. 270-274.

Appendix

A. Information on Test Scenes

The matrix used in Eric Haines' SPD database clipped out too much of the fractal mountain when it was generated at the resolution we chose (130 K polygons). Therefore, for comparison purposes, we provide the matrix we used here:

$$
\begin{bmatrix}
1.2 & 0 & 0 & 0 \\
0 & .297 & .742 & 0 \\
0 & .649 & -.259 & 0 \\
0 & .185 & 3.156 & 1
\end{bmatrix}
\tag{A.1}
$$

Also, the reader will note that the specified screen resolution which was proposed in the SPD database was 512 x 512, while our renderings were displayed at 640 x 484. The reason for this was that the algorithm used is intended as a scene development display algorithm for animation purposes and standard video resolution is 640 x 484. We expect that a resolution of 512 x 512 would result in somewhat similar timings.

B. Data for Various Algorithms

Each of the different implementations described in chapter 4 is presented in this section with the exact overhead percentages noted for each of the four test images. The algorithms are presented in the following order: scan line parallel, rectangular region (UD), rectangular region (LC), top-down, and task adaptive.

Scan line Data Non-Adaptive Algorithm

Scheduling
stegosaurus	0.01%
laser	0.006%
tree	0.005%
mount	0.002%

Memory Latency

	#remote refs	* 6.47 μsec	% of $Tp*P$
steg	5,765,541	37.3 sec	3.0%
laser	12,813,378	82.9 sec	4.0%
tree	15,250,407	98.7 sec	4.1%
mount	47,629,192	308.2 sec	5.6%

Switch Contention - 48 x 48 mesh

	$T(96)$	$T(1)$	% $Tp*P$	Calculated
steg	1036.99	834.22	16.2%	23.1%
laser	1818.50	1522.42	14.4%	17.9%
tree	2158.57	1973.95	7.8%	8.9%
mount	5199.22	4034.73	21.0%	20.5%

Load Imbalance - average over 3 runs

steg	10.4%
laser	8.1%
tree	8.7%
mountain	6.8%

Code Modification

	Time	% of $Tp*P$
steg	106.3 sec	8.5%
laser	157.7 sec	7.7%
tree	117.9 sec	4.9%
mount	543.9 sec	9.8%

Rectangular Data Non-Adaptive Algorithm (UD Scheme)

Scheduling
96 processors, 2304 areas

stegosaurus	0.013%
laser	0.009%
tree	0.007%
mountain	0.004%

Memory Latency

	remote refs	* 6.47 μsec	% of $Tp*P$
steg	2,677,256	17.32 sec	1.4%
laser	7,834,453	50.68 sec	2.6%
tree	12,395,847	80.20 sec	3.4%
mount	23,160,041	149.85 sec	3.6%

Code Modification

	Time Difference	% Total Proc-Time Space
steg	120.8 sec	8.7%
laser	164.6 sec	8.0%
tree	240.5 sec	9.6%
mount	341.6 sec	7.9%

Load Imbalance - average over 3 runs

steg	7.0%
laser	6.4%
tree	11.5%
mount	4.3%

Switch Contention - 48 x 48 mesh

	$T(96)$	$T(1)$	$\% Tp*P$	Calculated
steg	1087.16	828.81	18.7%	33.1%
laser	1800.05	1494.31	14.9%	20.6%
tree	2182.92	2074.59	4.3%	5.6%
mount	4053.71	3671.33	8.8%	10.9%

Rectangular Data Non-Adaptive Algorithm (LC Scheme)

Scheduling	2,304 areas
stegosaurus	0.017%
laser	0.01%
tree	0.007%
mountain	0.004%

Communication Overhead

	# bytes transferred	Time	$\% Tp*P$
steg	953,446	0.268 sec	0.028%
laser	2,288,116	0.644 sec	0.039%
tree	3,634,812	1.022 sec	0.047%
mount	6,788,070	1.909 sec	0.052%

Load Imbalance - average over 3 runs

steg	6.8%
laser	6.6%
tree	11.1%
mount	4.5%

Code Modification

	Time Difference	% $Tp*P$
steg	62.3 sec	6.4%
laser	103.0 sec	6.3%
tree	119.6 sec	5.5%
mount	196.4 sec	5.4%

Switch Contention - 48 x 48 mesh

	$T(96)$	$T(1)$	% $Tp*P$	Calculated
steg	881.26	753.14	13.1%	16.3%
laser	1502.99	1385.45	7.2%	8.9%
tree	1940.51	1877.89	2.9%	3.1%
mount	3485.53	3380.91	2.9%	3.2%

Data Adaptive Top-Down Decomposition

Scheduling, 960 regions

stegosaurus	0.01%
laser	0.007%
tree	0.006%
mountain	0.003%

Communication Overhead

	# bytes transferred	Time	% $Tp*P$
steg	653,060	0.18 sec	0.02 %
laser	1,833,368	0.52 sec	0.03 %
tree	3,110,170	0.87 sec	0.04 %
mount	5,654,696	1.59 sec	0.04 %

Load Imbalance - average over 3 runs

steg	1.5%
laser	6.9%
tree	4.0%
mount	3.1%

Code Modification

	Time Difference	% $Tp*P$
steg	32.3 sec	2.8 %
laser	59.1 sec	3.3 %
tree	59.9 sec	2.6 %
mount	97.9 sec	2.5 %

Switch Contention - 48 x 48 mesh

	$T(96)$	$T(1)$	% $Tp*P$	Calculated
steg	1109.4	723.0	34.0 %	34.9 %
laser	1649.5	1341.4	17.4 %	17.3 %
tree	2177.9	1818.2	15.7 %	16.9 %
mount	3736.6	3282.1	11.8 %	11.8 %

Task Adaptive Algorithm

Number of Tasks

	non-background tasks	total tasks
steg	209	254
laser	183	235
tree	233	245
mount	224	243

Scheduling

stegosaurus	0.00023%
laser	0.00014%
tree	0.0001%
mountain	0.00006%

Communication Overhead

	# bytes transferred	Time	% $Tp*P$
steg	3,876,924	1.1 sec	0.11 %
laser	251,191,547	70.7 sec	4.20 %
tree	21,747,484	6.1 sec	0.25 %
mount	19,765,530	5.6 sec	0.15 %

Load Imbalance - average over 3 runs

steg	14.3%
laser	10.3%
tree	22.5%
mount	9.2%

Code Modification

	Time Difference	% $Tp*P$
steg	3.9 sec	0.4 %
laser	25.6 sec	1.6 %
tree	17.6 sec	0.7 %
mount	31.5 sec	0.8 %

Switch Contention - 48 x 48 mesh

	$T(96)$	$T(1)$	$\% Tp*P$	Calculated
steg	798.7 sec	695.6 sec	10.6 %	11.7 %
laser	1489.5 sec	1309.7 sec	10.2 %	9.2 %
tree	1900.4 sec	1781.0 sec	4.8 %	5.6 %
mount	3433.8 sec	3219.7 sec	5.7 %	5.5 %

Synchronization

	Time	$\% Tp*P$
steg	21.2 sec	2.2 %
laser	39.4 sec	2.3 %
tree	4.0 sec	0.16 %
mount	7.9 sec	0.21 %

C. Supplementary Graphs

Additional graphs are given here for the purpose of providing a better evaluation of the various algorithms. These graphs, listed in order of appearance, are the following:

1. Ratio Comparison for Rectangular Region Decomposition, UD Scheme
2. Ratio Comparison for Rectangular Region Decomposition, LC Scheme
3. Duplication Factors vs. Number of Areas
4. Comparison of Operating Systems for GP1000, Rectangular Region, UD Scheme
5. Comparison of Operating Systems for GP1000, Rectangular Region, LC Scheme
6. Comparison of All Algorithms, Total Time including Tiling and Front End, High resolution on the GP1000
7. Comparison of All Algorithms, Total Time including Tiling and Front End, High resolution on the TC2000

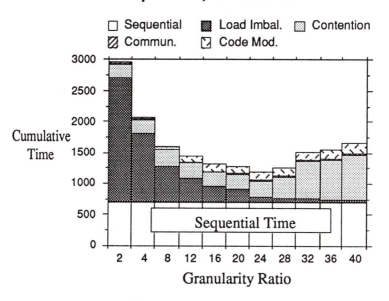

Figure A.1: Comparison of ratios for stegosaurus image, UD

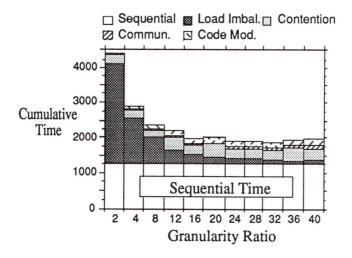

Figure A.2: Comparison of ratios for Laser image, UD

Ratio Comparison for Rectangular Region Decomposition, UD Scheme

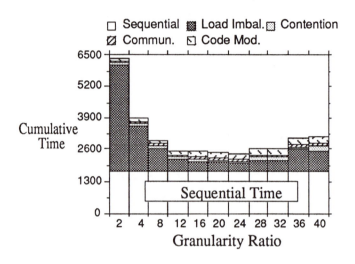

Figure A.3: Comparison of ratios for tree image, UD

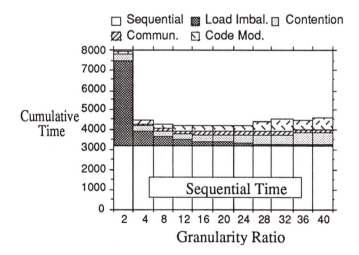

Figure A.4: Comparison of ratios for mountain image, UD

Ratio Comparison for Rectangular Region Decomposition, LC Scheme

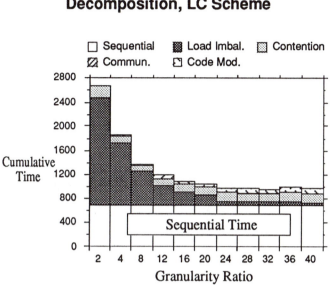

Figure A.5: Comparison of ratios for stegosaurus image, LC

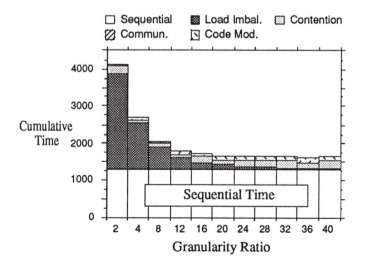

Figure A.6: Comparison of ratios for Laser image, LC

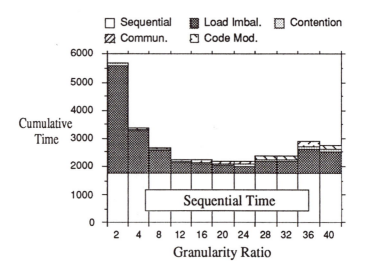

Figure A.7: Comparison of ratios for tree image, LC

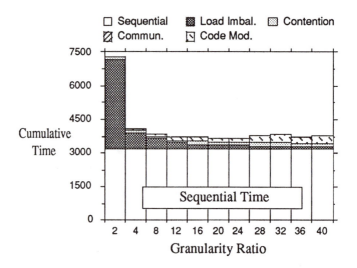

Figure A.8: Comparison of ratios for mountain image, LC

Duplication Factors vs. Number of Areas

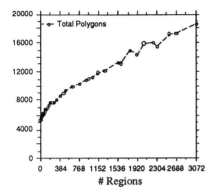

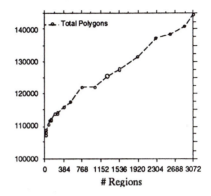

Figure A.9: Total polygons versus
number of areas, stegosaurus image

Figure A.11: Total polygons versus
number of areas, tree image

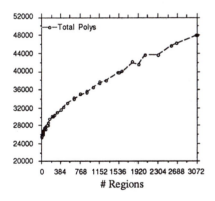

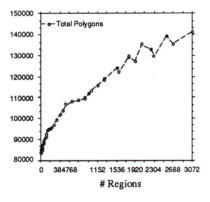

Figure A.10: Total polygons versus
number of areas, Laser image

Figure A.12: Total polygons versus
number of areas, mountain image

Comparison of Operating Systems for GP1000
Rectangular Region, UD Scheme

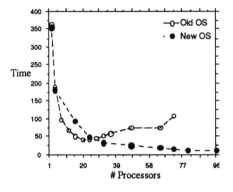

Figure A.13: Comparison of old OS
vs. new OS for stegosaurus image,
rectangular region UD

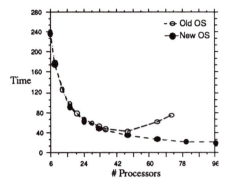

Figure A.15: Comparison of old OS
vs. new OS for Laser image,
rectangular region UD

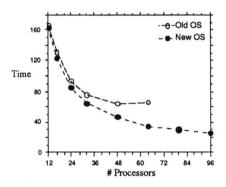

Figure A.14: Comparison of old OS
vs. new OS for tree image,
rectangular region UD

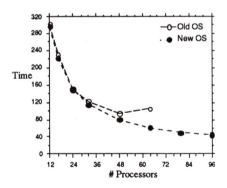

Figure A.16: Comparison of old OS
vs. new OS for mountain image,
rectangular region UD

Comparison of Operating Systems for GP1000, Rectangular Region, LC Scheme

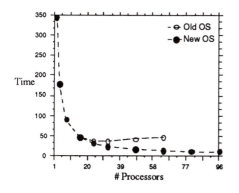

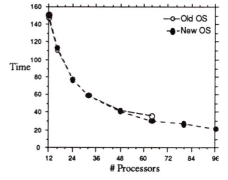

Figure A.17: Comparison of old OS vs. new OS for stegosaurus image, rectangular region LC

Figure A.19: Comparison of old OS vs. new OS for tree image, rectangular region LC

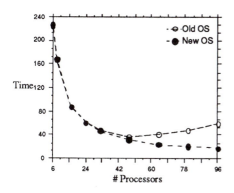

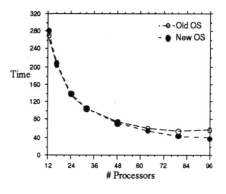

Figure A.18: Comparison of old OS vs. new OS for Laser image, rectangular region LC

Figure A.20: Comparison of old OS vs. new OS for mountain image, rectangular region LC

Comparison of algorithms, total time including tiling + fe, high-res, GP1000

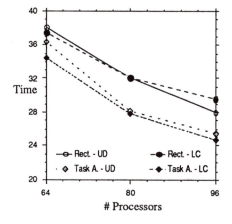

Figure A.21: Total time comparison, GP1000, stegosaurus image, hi-res

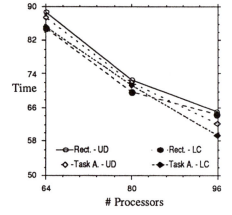

Figure A.23: Total time comparison, GP1000, tree image, hi-res

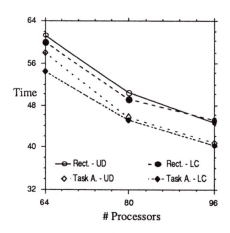

Figure A.22: Total time comparison, GP1000, Laser image, hi-res

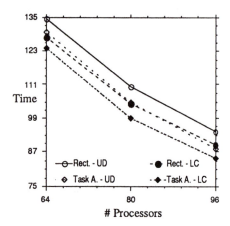

Figure A.24: Total time comparison, GP1000, mountain image, hi-res

Comparison of algorithms, total time including tiling + fe, high-res, TC2000

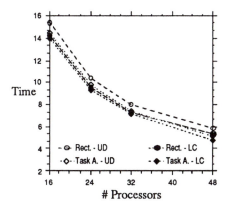

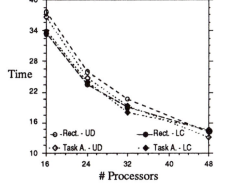

Figure A.25: Total time comparison, TC2000, stegosaurus image, hi-res

Figure A.27: Total time comparison, TC2000, tree image, hi-res

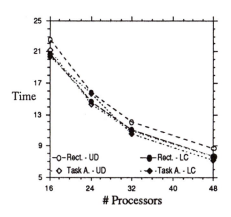

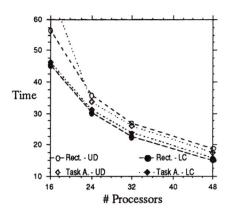

Figure A.26: Total time comparison, TC2000, Laser image, hi-res

Figure A.28: Total time comparison, TC2000, mountain image, hi-res

Index

Jones and Bartlett Books in Computer Science and Related Areas

Barnsley, M., *The Fractal Transform*
ISBN 0-86720-218-1

Bernstein, A.J., and Lewis, P.M., *Concurrency in Programming and Database Systems*
ISBN 0-86720-205-X

Birmingham, W.P., Gupta, A.P., and Siewiorek, D., *Automating the Design of Computer Systems: The MICON Project*
ISBN 0-86720-241-6

Chandy, K.M., and Taylor, S., *An Introduction to Parallel Programming*
ISBN 0-86720-208-4

Epstein, D.B.A., *et al., Word Processing in Groups*
ISBN 0-86720-241-6

Flynn, A., and Jones, J., *Mobile Robots: Inspiration to Implementation*
ISBN 0-86720-223-8

Geometry Center, University of Minnesota, *Not Knot* (VHS video)
ISBN 0-86720-240-8

Iterated Systems, Inc., *Floppy Book: A P.OEM PC Book*
ISBN 0-86720-222-X

Iterated Systems, Inc., *SNAPSHOTS: True-Color Photo Images Using the Fractal Formatter*
ISBN 0-86720-299-8

Lee, E. S., *Algorithms and Data Structures in Computer Engineering*
ISBN 0-86720-219-X

Meyers, B.A. (ed.), *Languages for Developing User Interfaces*
ISBN 0-86720-450-8

Parke, F.I., and Waters, K., *Computer Facial Animation*
ISBN 0-86720-243-2

Ruskai, M.B., *et al., Wavelets and Their Applications*
ISBN 0-86720-225-4

Whitman, S., *Multiprocessor Methods for Computer Graphics Rendering*
ISBN 0-86720-229-7